PAY UP!

Unlocking Insider Secrets of Salary Negotiation

KATE DIXON

Oceanside Press • Portland, Oregon

So. The legalese.

I give advice and counsel, combined with opinions, notions, and hypotheses gathered from many (many!) years of experience. That said, none of what I say, write, teach, or believe should substitute for your own judgement and/or good sense.

While some of the work I do with clients can seem like magic, it really isn't. It's the combination of my clients' motivation, hard work, insights, and dedication, plus a good bit of perspective coming from me.

Even though these techniques work for my clients, they may not work for you. I do not guarantee your outcomes or results. It's really up to you, and how (and when and how hard) you choose to apply what you learn. It is my hope that reading these success stories will help motivate and inspire you to achieve your own personal successes. You are responsible for your own choices, actions, and results.

This book is only for informational and educational purposes and should not be considered therapy or any form of treatment. The information contained in this book is accurate to the best of my knowledge at the time of publishing. References are provided for informational purposes only, and readers should be aware that the websites listed in this book may change. While every attempt has been made to verify the information provided here, neither I, my publisher, nor our collective affiliates or partners, assume any responsibility for errors, inaccuracies, or omissions, whether such errors or omissions result from negligence, accident or another cause. We specifically disclaim any warranties (implied or otherwise) and shall in no event be liable for any loss of profit or any other loss or damage, including, but not limited to special, incidental, consequential, or other damages, whether direct or indirect.

Publisher's Cataloging-in-Publication Data

Names: Dixon, Kate, author.
Title: Pay up! : unlocking insider secrets of salary negotiation / Kate Dixon.
Description: Portland, OR : Oceanside Press, 2020. | Includes index.
Identifiers: LCCN 2020915257 (print) | ISBN 978-1-7346992-6-5 (paperback) | ISBN 978-1-7346992-1-0 (hardcover) | ISBN 978-1-7346992-0-3 (ebook)
Subjects: LCSH: Wages. | Negotiation. | Negotiation in business. | Job offers. | Employment interviewing. | BISAC: BUSINESS & ECONOMICS / Negotiating. | BUSINESS & ECONOMICS / Careers / Job Hunting.
Classification: LCC HF5549.5.I6 D59 2020 (print) | LCC HF5549.5.I6 (ebook) DDC 650.14--dc23.

For Steve, Liz, and Jay

Contents

Introduction

Negotiating your salary can be terrifying. There are so many things to get wrong, you may not even know when you're doing it right.

I understand that fear. If this will be your first time negotiating pay, your anxiety is probably off the charts. And if you've negotiated before, just knowing how much could be on the line can be breathtakingly scary.

Here's a secret: ***pay negotiation doesn't have to be scary.***

What if I told you that you could:

- Get tools and information about pay to make great decisions
- Learn skills to negotiate, including what to say (and what NOT to)

- Shift your mindset and be more confident and powerful during negotiations?

Guess what? ***You can.***

I've coached clients on salary negotiation at all levels, from college undergraduates to top level (C-suite) executives. And I've worked for and consulted with all kinds of organizations on compensation, too. From nonprofits to startups to Fortune 100 companies, I've seen (and designed) just about every sort of pay practice there is. And I want to help you get more confident and competent — and get more of what you want and less of what you don't.

This book will help you understand — and negotiate — your entire pay package (including pay, benefits, and relocation), whether it's your first job out of school or it's your last job before retirement.

To succeed in any sort of pay negotiation you need great tools and skills, plus the right mindset to give you the best chance at success. This book will absolutely help you do all three of those things. And I'll answer the most common questions my salary negotiation clients (and complete strangers!) ask me.

WHY SHOULD YOU NEGOTIATE PAY?

In the U.S., negotiating is expected, especially at higher levels of the organization. The fact that lots of other people don't doesn't mean you shouldn't!

Negotiating your pay certainly won't count against you, either, as long as you're not a jerk (more on that later). Why not try it?

A 2019 study by Jobvite found that 83% of job seekers who tried to negotiate pay were able to get higher pay (and 34% of those got more than a 10% increase!). Even if you don't get additional money or better employment terms as a result of your negotiation (and I bet you will), it's valuable to get experience with pay negotiation. The more you do it, the more comfortable and effective you'll be.

WHAT YOU'LL LEARN

Some of the cool stuff you'll learn in this book includes:

- What **information you need** to get when you're preparing for your negotiation (and where to get it)
- What those **compensation and benefit terms** really mean, and which ones you can negotiate
- How to figure out **what you're leaving behind** with your current employer, and how to leverage that into more money and/or equity
- How to sort through your offer to **really understand** it
- **Best practices** in pay negotiation
- **What to say** (and what not to) in your negotiations
- How to **end your conversations** with your recruiter or hiring manager
- What you **should *never do*** in your negotiations
- The role your **clarity** plays in your negotiation process
- How to step back and **not take things personally** (it can be done!)

- How to shift your mindset and **get out of your own way**
- The best way to **prepare** for your negotiation conversations
- …and how to put everything together so you're **at your best** in your negotiations!

I'M SUPER-SMART AND BUSINESS-SAVVY! WHY DO I NEED SALARY NEGOTIATION ADVICE?

I get this question a lot. The truth of the matter is salary negotiation is hard.

It's hard because it can be emotional. It's hard because many of us have been socialized not to advocate for ourselves financially. It's hard because it involves money. And it's hard because it involves a technical discipline most people have never been exposed to before. Plus, everyone thinks they should already know how to do it, so they don't spend time learning and preparing.

Trust me. You don't want to just bumble through.

Smart, business-savvy folks need this book because…

You're nervous about salary negotiation.

Yup! You're nervous because this is a big deal! The thing to remember is that both you and the person you're negotiating pay with both want the same thing: for you to come to work for the company and for you to be happy about it (because they've offered you the job, you can assume *they're* happy about it). Just knowing you have that common ground can make the process less nerve-racking. At least a little.

And the more you know about how all of this works, the more confident — and competent — you'll become.

You don't know what you don't know.

You're not supposed to be a compensation expert (unless you are, then see below). The person negotiating pay with you knows that.

But you do need to be informed (be prepared to geek out!) and know how to ask good questions. There are tons of those here, too.

> Negotiating your pay won't count against you as long as you're **not a jerk.**

You know too much.

There's such a thing as knowing too much. Those of us with backgrounds designing pay programs or negotiating pay from the talent acquisition side know oodles about how companies pay people. And we might get our brains bent by trying to figure out exactly what's going on behind the proverbial curtains.

If you know more than your fair share, just stop. We'll talk about how to get out of your own way in the Mindset section, which will help lots if you're in this situation.

You have no clue what to ask for.

Whether this is your first rodeo or your tenth, there are likely to be things you haven't considered, or items you don't know to ask for. And companies will often ask you what you want before they tell you what they're going to offer.

Your job is to understand at least a bit about the market for the job you're looking at, and to know what's important to you.

The best thing you can do here is to make sure you do your homework. You'll get great tips on what different parts of your package really mean, what's common to negotiate, and how things typically work inside of companies.

You don't actually think you deserve what you're asking for.

Especially if you've got self-esteem issues or if you're negotiating with an organization with a strong social mission, this can be a real sticking point.

Remember, you've got a great background and expertise the organization needs, or you wouldn't have the job offer. Of course, don't let that take you over the top to obnoxious; calm confidence works well.

What you've tried before hasn't worked.

Nobody nails it on the first try (at least not without the tools you'll learn here). If you've tried — and failed — with salary negotiations in the past, you could use some help to figure out a successful game plan. The most common salary negotiation fails are:

- Going in without knowing what you want ("more of everything" isn't a strategy)
- Going in without a game plan (just because you think well on your feet doesn't mean you shouldn't prepare)

- Going in with a chip on your shoulder (salary negotiation is *not* the Hunger Games, and it's definitely not personal)

You'll find so many strategies, ideas, and tactics that work for my clients here, you'll never have to use your tried-and-un-true ways again.

You're worried they'll withdraw the offer.

Don't worry. Really. Companies expect you to negotiate, as long as you do it in good faith (and aren't a jerk). I've never in my very long career seen an offer withdrawn because a candidate negotiated their offer.

You just want it to be over.

I hear you! But stick with it – negotiating pay can't actually go on forever, even if it seems like it does sometimes. If you can focus on that great new job waiting for you on the other side, the momentary discomfort of negotiating your pay package won't be so bad.

And once you've done your prep and practiced what you're going to say, the prospect of a negotiation conversation won't seem so intimidating. I promise!

You know you need help.

Yes, you do! I'll be with you every step of the way, from getting ready even before you get the offer all the way to the after-party.

WHO THIS BOOK IS FOR

If you're planning a move to a job at another (or your first) company this book is a great starting point. While a lot of advice in the book can be used when you're negotiating pay at your current organization, it was designed for people changing companies.

If you're curious about how things work, you're willing to reflect on what's important to you, and you take the time to plan and prepare, you're in the best position to benefit from ***Pay UP!***

My engaged, self-aware, and dedicated clients get the very best results from salary negotiation coaching, and they're the kind of folks I wrote this book for.

WHO THIS BOOK IS *NOT* FOR

If you think that pay negotiation is a zero-sum game with one winner and one loser, you won't find much to reinforce your perspective here. That whole "I-win-you-lose" thing won't get you what you want over the long term. Stick with me, and you'll find out why.

Likewise, if you're looking for a quick fix that doesn't require any thinking or introspection or practice, this isn't the book for you.

HOW THIS BOOK IS STRUCTURED

I've divided ***Pay UP!*** into four sections to make things easy for you:

1. **Toolset.** These are the tools and the information you need to make great decisions. I'll break down all of the elements in your pay package, talk about what you can and can't negotiate, and tell you exactly where you can get market data and the other info you need to get started.

2. **Skillset.** You'll find the skills you must develop to negotiate well in this section. You'll learn what questions to ask to understand your offer, get the basics of negotiation, and find out exactly what to say – and what to avoid at all costs.
3. **Mindset.** This section will help you set your intention for your negotiations and get out of your own way. We'll cover getting clear about what you want, shifting your mindset, and learning how not to take salary negotiation personally (which is a bigger deal than you might think).
4. **Putting It All Together.** You'll learn how to create your game plan and prepare for your negotiations. We'll also talk about special circumstances that might affect your negotiation, and what you should do when you're done.

Also, each section has a Client Success Story plus Q&As to illustrate how things come to life.

HOW TO USE THIS BOOK

This book is a resource meant to spark ideas and to arm you with knowledge and resources to do a great job for yourself.

It's not a crutch or a cure-all. It's not a substitute for good judgement, and it can't take into consideration everything that's special about your situation.

Pay UP! provides insights, stories, and actionable steps to prepare you for your salary negotiations and help you become more confident and competent when talking about pay with others.

Let's get to it!

PART 1

TOOLSET

Your Toolset is the information and tools you need to make great decisions. This covers elements like what the competitive landscape looks like for the job you're looking at, what sorts of things are common in a pay package, and what's common to negotiate (and what isn't).

Really understanding what you're getting (and getting into) is one of the most important parts of negotiating pay. If you don't understand the elements that make up your package, you can't possibly appreciate or value them. Trust me: your employer wants you to value every single thing they're giving you!

What's in this section…

Chapter 1: Resources

Where you can find resources for market data about jobs, as well as internal pay practices and information about the organization.

Chapter 2: What's in Total Rewards?

Explanations of common elements of total rewards, including compensation, benefits, relocation, and other stuff.

Chapter 3: Cost of Living vs. Cost of Labor

Understanding the difference between how much it costs to live in a place vs. how much you get paid there. Remote work and market comparisons.

Chapter 4: What Can (and Can't) You Negotiate?

Most commonly negotiated pay elements. What's typically more difficult to negotiate.

Chapter 5: Toolset Client Success Story

How one of my clients used the ***Pay UP!*** Toolset to effectively negotiate a transition from a mid-management role in a large company to an executive role in a smaller one.

Chapter 6: Toolset Q&A

Questions I get about stuff in the Toolset section (and how I answer them).

Chapter 1
Resources

The first part of our toolset is all about your resources — the data and information you need to make your best decisions.

EXTERNAL SALARY DATA

You need to familiarize yourself with pay practices for your level and type of job (and sometimes, your industry). This step is crucial for anyone negotiating an external offer (one that comes from a company you're not currently working for).

The great news is that there are more sources now than ever before! But that's the bad news, too — it's hard to know where to turn.

Online sources. First off, check out online sources. This includes Glassdoor.com, Salary.com, and job search engines like Indeed.com and Monster.com. Make sure you're matching your search as closely as possible to the job duties of your prospective job, and keep in mind the size of the organization. Job titles can vary (tons!) from place to place, and a VP job at a huge company will likely pay more than a VP job at a small organization.

Professional organizations. Professional organizations, like ones for attorneys, or nurses, or corporate trainers, or plumbers often sponsor salary surveys, and share the data with their members. If you belong to an organization that's function- or job-specific, be sure to ask if they have pay data available; when they do, it's often tucked away as a special benefit for members.

Annual reports. If you're a senior executive, a great source of compensation data for publicly traded companies is annual reports. The CD&A (or Compensation Discussion and Analysis) is a required part of the proxy, and it has a treasure trove of great info about executive pay in general, and Named Executive Officer pay, in particular.

Want to know about what executive bonuses are based on? Got it. Which pay elements top execs get? Bingo. And sometimes, there are gems like offer letters and entire employment agreements in or around the CD&A, too.

Social media. You can also check out social media – people tweet and post about pay studies and other sources pretty regularly.

Friends and colleagues. Don't forget to ask your friends and colleagues about market pay. It's a lot more common to talk openly about pay now than it was even five years ago.

Feel weird? You can always start the conversation like this: "I'm collecting information about pay for jobs like you have, and my research is showing salaries in the $XX to $YY range." (A good rule of thumb is to make the top of the range about 10% higher than the bottom.) "Would you mind telling me if you're in/above/under that range?" If they're hesitant to share that info, you can ask them if the range sounds right to them, instead.

The great news is that there are **more sources for external salary data** than ever before.

INTERNAL REWARDS DATA

You should absolutely know what your current company's pay package and policies are (and don't forget benefits!). It's important information when you're looking externally for a job.

Why? Because when you change companies, you simply must know what you're leaving behind. The more you know about what you have — and how things work — the better job of negotiation you can do.

If you work for a large organization, there's bound to be tons of information about how things work on the company intranet. Sometimes, training for managers on awarding merit, bonuses, and equity is available to all employees (sometimes not, though). Be curious, keep your eyes open, and ask lots of questions.

ORGANIZATION INFORMATION

You'll also want to do your research about the organization you have an offer from. Most companies, even smaller ones, have a page dedicated to what it's like to work for them (it'll be linked to their careers/jobs page). These pages will typically share information about locations, company culture, their commitment to diversity, and if you're lucky, pay and benefits.

Some of the larger companies will also share details about their benefits packages, which can be awesome background. Of course, once you get your offer, you'll get tons more information.

A side note on company culture: don't just take the website's word for it. Asking questions of current (and former) employees about company culture — and how it stacks up to the promise from the website — can help you know if the organization's right for you. Or not.

OFFER LETTER

Your offer letter as a source of data? Heck yeah!

Pore over everything that comes with your offer letter/ email. There will usually be information about benefits (and relocation and equity, if applicable). And information about the company itself. Lots of great stuff.

If you're in the fortunate position to be comparing offers, really knowing what's in all of your offer letters and attachments can help you compare and contrast.

EXPERT ADVICE

Seek out books specific to your industry, blog posts, and other expert information to help you discover what you don't already know. If you're negotiating a complicated employment agreement or startup equity, you may want to talk with an attorney; when making choices about deferred compensation, you'll probably want to chat with your financial planner.

If you're still struggling with the whole idea of pay negotiation (or just certain parts of it) after reading this book, there are salary negotiation coaches for that (like me!).

It makes way more sense to invest in getting expert advice before you accept an offer — it could save you (or get you) big bucks.

PRO TIPS

- Gather salary data from several sources, and don't hesitate to ask peers.
- Knowing your current company's pay practices is essential to good salary negotiation.
- Look to online information and ask questions of employees to understand pay and culture information in a prospective company.
- Your offer letter has great information about rewards. Read it. All of it.
- You may need an expert to help you navigate some of the less-standard aspects of your offer.

Chapter 2

What's in Total Rewards?

Let's go into more depth about what might be included in your total rewards (also known as "compensation and benefits") package. Some of these items are more common at certain levels in the organization (like long-term incentives), some of them are more common with a specific type of job (like sales commissions), and you definitely won't find all of these elements in any single job.

I've broken these down into groups: Pay, Benefits, Relocation, and Other Stuff. And let me begin by saying that these are general rules of thumb. You need to pay close attention to your offer letter and/or employment contract; they may specify things that are different than what you see in this book.

You might be tempted to write to me and say, "Hey, Kate! The way you described <fill in the name of whatever pay or benefit> isn't exactly like what I got offered." That will happen. This is just meant to give a broad overview, not account for every single variation you might come across.

Compensation

Compensation covers so much more than base pay. It includes everything from bonuses, to differentials, to long-term cash, to equity.

Many folks believe that base pay is the only thing you should negotiate in your offer. And while it's the most commonly negotiated, there are lots of other things you should know before you decide what exactly you want to negotiate.

BASE PAY AND DIFFERENTIALS

Base Pay. For folks below the executive level, base pay is the biggest part of your pie. Whether you're paid hourly or you're salaried, this is the "meat and potatoes" of your take-home pay each pay period. Base pay is typically expressed as an annual figure in your offer letter for salaried employees and an hourly figure for those who are eligible for overtime.

Geographic Differentials. In high cost of labor areas (like New York City and San Francisco), companies sometimes will offer an additional line item as an addition to base pay. This typically happens when someone is likely to move between locations so that the differential can be easily removed when they move to a lower cost of labor area.

These aren't very common anymore, and when they do show up, they're more likely to be in lower-level jobs. For most people in high cost of labor areas, the differential is already "baked into" higher pay ranges and higher base pay.

Shift Differentials. These are most common for folks who are eligible for overtime, but you could see them in any role that requires you to work nonstandard hours on a regular basis. They're usually expressed as an additional percentage of your base pay or an additional amount per hour, and they show up as a separate line item in your paycheck. But not every job that requires nonstandard work hours offers shift differentials, so be sure to ask.

CASH INCENTIVES AND INCREASES

Annual bonus/incentive. Your annual bonus opportunity is typically expressed as a percent of your annual base pay. So, if your base pay is $50,000 and your bonus target is 10% (and you're there for the whole year, etc.), you could expect to get somewhere in the neighborhood of $5,000 at the end of the annual performance period. Whether it's more or less will depend on what the performance measures for your plan are and how you/your team/your company performed.

Commissions. These are normal for sales roles but aren't typical for other sorts of jobs. And when you're eligible for commission, you're typically not eligible for other types of annual incentives or bonuses. (But sometimes, you are, so check your offer letter!)

Commissions are incentives for selling products or services. They're typically expressed as a ratio of base pay to commission. So, a 70/30 split with a $70,000 base would mean the commission target would be $30,000. Commissions are often paid out more frequently than the annual bonus. The most common commission payout timing I've seen is quarterly, but I've seen everything from monthly to annual.

Profit Sharing. Profit sharing programs share a portion of the company's profits, usually annually, with employees. Each program is a little different, but it's pretty normal to have the amount of your share of the profits tied to your level in the company or your base pay.

Cost of Living Adjustments. Cost of living adjustments (or COLAs, for short) are pretty rare these days. We see them most often in government jobs and in union environments. These increases to base pay are designed to respond to inflation, and they typically don't have any tie to performance (although sometimes people become ineligible for COLAs if they have poor performance).

Merit Pay. Some people think merit pay and COLAs are the same thing, but they're not. Merit pay is meant to reward employees for successful and outstanding performance. And in general, the higher the performance, the bigger the increase. If you're already high in the pay range, even if you're a strong performer, you may not get a big increase (or if you get one, it might be in the form of a "lump sum" and not added into your base pay).

Merit pay is almost always on an annual cycle, and most companies have a common date that they give out all of their merit increases. We'll talk more about negotiating your review date later in the book.

Timing of Next Pay Review. One of the things I encourage my clients to talk with prospective employers about, especially when they're not able to negotiate their base pay as high as they'd like at the offer stage, is the timing of their next pay review. You can ask for a review of your pay six months (or sometimes even three months) after you start working for your new company and have a chance to show them how awesome your results are.

While base pay is the most commonly negotiated compensation element, there are **lots of other items** you may want to negotiate.

EQUITY AND LONG-TERM INCENTIVES

Please note: equity rules and vesting schedules vary greatly between companies, and you absolutely must know the particulars of how your plan works. Read your plan document carefully, and if you don't understand it, ask questions (or hire an advisor to help you) so that you're really clear.

Stock Options. Stock options are part of a group of rewards called "long-term incentives." This means that it takes a long time to get their full value. They're designed to encourage you to stay with the company over the long term.

A stock option is the *right to buy* a share of the company for a certain price (the "grant price"), which is set when the company grants it to you. You get value when the exercise price (which is the price of the stock when you sell it) is higher than the grant price.

There's no value in a stock option unless the stock price increases; on the other hand, you don't have to pay anything if the stock price falls below the grant price.

Options vest over time (usually somewhere between three and five years), and most plans have some sort of partial vesting along the way. Oh, and "vesting" is just a fancy way to say that you get the thing over time.

For example, if your equity vests 25% per year over four years, and you leave between year two and three, you'll have vested 50% (which you get to exercise) and the remaining 50% you forfeit.

Restricted Stock. Restricted Stock is another long-term incentive. This is when the company grants you actual shares of stock, which you vest in over time. The cool thing about restricted stock is that its value is the value of the actual stock, so it's easier to understand. And if the price of the stock stays the same or goes down, you'll still get some value when you exercise (sell) it. Which can only happen after it vests, of course.

Restricted Stock (or Share) Units. RSUs act just like restricted stock, but they're not actual shares, just the value of the shares.

Long-Term Cash. Yet another long-term incentive, long-term cash offers a cash payout for long-term performance. Most of these plans are between three and five years long. It's important to read the plan documents to understand the details of your plan, especially to make sure you know how the first few years are handled.

Deferred Compensation. Deferred comp programs offer you the opportunity to earmark a part of your earnings for a future year. You pick the amount to defer and the year you want to receive those earnings (and pay taxes on them). Most people choose to receive their deferred comp in retirement, when they might be paying a lower tax rate, or in a year they anticipate large expenses, like college tuition or buying a house. It's common for companies to have a base pay threshold to participate, or only offer it to executive employees.

SIGN-ON BONUS/EQUITY

Sign-on Bonus. This is a cash bonus that's paid soon after you're hired, and it's meant to be an enticement to move to the new company. Companies will often use sign-on bonuses to cover relocation expenses or to make up for an annual bonus or long-term incentives that you're walking away from in your old company.

Sign-on Equity. Like sign-on bonuses, some companies use equity (stock options or restricted stock) to encourage candidates to accept the new job. Sign-on equity is common for startup companies, and it's also used a lot for technical positions in tech companies.

PRO TIPS

- Base pay is the biggest component of total rewards for most jobs. Executives and some sales professionals are the exception.
- There are lots of different types of bonuses and incentives that companies offer, and you should understand what you're getting.
- Long-term incentives, including long-term cash and equity awards, typically make up the biggest share of total rewards for executives, and they can also be a big component of pay for tech pay packages.

Benefits

Clients ask me all the time why they should even bother negotiating the benefits side of things, since it's not as common to negotiate most of the things on this list.

There's a huge reason: benefits differ a ton from one organization to the next, and it's crucial for you to know how things work. Not only so you can take advantage of all of the benefits you're offered, but so you can use what you learn to negotiate other things (like base pay or sign-on cash) more effectively.

INSURANCE

When you're looking at insurance benefits, there are two main things to consider: 1) What the premiums cost (the amount you have to pay per paycheck for the benefit), and 2) What is covered. A really inexpensive premium can seem like a great idea, until you discover how much you have to pay out of pocket for services.

If you have ongoing health concerns, have high prescription costs, or anticipate a major health-related event (like a surgery or a pregnancy), you can (and should) ask to speak with an expert from the insurance company — even before you accept the offer — to understand how the company's policy will impact you. Under healthcare privacy laws, the insurance company will not be able to share any of the content of your discussions with your future employer.

Healthcare Insurance. This is the insurance you use to pay for doctor visits, hospitalizations, and prescriptions.

Dental Insurance. You'll use dental insurance to get your teeth cleaned, get cavities filled, pay for braces, and other stuff. Just so you know, cosmetic services like teeth whitening or veneers will almost never be covered under dental insurance.

Vision Insurance. Vision insurance typically covers regular eye exams, glasses, and contacts.

Prescription Drug Insurance. This insurance helps pay for prescription medications. The amount of coverage can vary widely, so if you take prescription medicine (especially those that are expensive and/or needed daily), you'll want to understand your coverage.

Life insurance. Life insurance pays money to your beneficiaries (people you select) when you die. Companies often cover a minimal amount of life insurance (typically equal to one year of base pay) with no cost to you, and allow you to purchase more up to a set multiplier of your salary.

Many organizations also allow you to cover your spouse and sometimes your dependents with life insurance, too.

AD&D. AD&D stands for "Accidental Death and Dismemberment" insurance. Sounds creepy, but this kind of insurance can be especially important if you have a family who depends on your income or if you wouldn't be able to work after losing use of a limb.

RETIREMENT PROGRAMS

401(k) Programs. Most companies these days offer 401(k) plans (or their equivalents, in nonprofit orgs) to their employees, which allow them to set aside pre-tax income to invest for their retirement.

Lots of companies offer a "match" (where the employer contributes an amount equal to your contributions to your account) up to a certain percentage. For example, if a company has a 3% match, and you contribute 3% of your pay into your 401(k), this means you'd actually have 6% of your pay set aside. Which is awesome! One thing to note: most employer matches vest over time — sometimes as much as five years — so if you leave before that time, you could forfeit some or all of your match money.

Other Retirement Programs. Pension plans are largely a thing of the past, but if you're offered one, get the details. They're so uncommon that you're not likely to run into peers who can tell you much about them! And government retirement programs are unique to themselves. When you get an offer from a governmental agency, it's likely that they'll tell you lots about their retirement plans, since they're often a big draw for those types of jobs.

PAID TIME OFF

Holidays. I'm not lumping this in with vacation, since it's really its own separate thing. And organizations are all over the place with holidays. Some have very few, others shut down operations between Christmas and New Year's, and some have all federal holidays off. It's great to know so you have a good understanding of all of your potential days off.

Vacation and Paid Time Off (PTO). Just like with holidays, companies have wildly different vacation and paid time off policies. Some companies have "unlimited time off" (pro tip: ask people how that comes to life in that particular organization; it sounds awesome, but sometimes it means "nobody takes much vacation because we all feel weird about it").

Benefits **differ a ton** from one organization to the next, and it's crucial for you to know how things work.

In most organizations, you'll accrue time off, earning a certain number of hours per pay period, adding up to the yearly amount by the end of a full year. In others, you get your full-year allocation at the beginning of the year.

It's great to know how vacation/paid time off changes over time, too. A company that gives one week of PTO in the first year, and three weeks every year after might be a better bet than a company that gives two weeks forever and ever.

In any case, you'll eventually want to know what the policy looks like for rolling over unused time so you don't lose any of your precious time off. It's not a typical discussion in the offer negotiation process, though.

Sick Leave. Some companies don't have sick leave at all and expect you to take sick days out of your PTO pool. Others allow you to take some number of days off when you're sick (and don't expect that you'll use those days to take vacation). It's good to know what's what.

Parental/Family Leave. Parental and family leaves allow employees to take paid time off for the birth of a child, adoption, or to care for a sick or injured family member. Programs can vary greatly from place to place, so it's good to do your homework here, especially if you plan on having kids or if you anticipate you may need to care for a family member while you're employed.

Sabbatical. A sabbatical is a program that usually offers extended time off with pay. Programs I've seen range from five to twelve weeks, and employees become eligible after an extended period of service. I personally love the sabbatical concept, but since you have to stay at a company for a long time to get one, it may or may not be something that you value in a pay package. Sabbatical programs are not at all common, so don't expect to see them in every company.

OTHER BENEFITS

Employee Stock Purchase Plan (ESPP). ESPPs allow employees to purchase company stock at a discounted price. Terms of ESPPs can vary quite a bit, so don't assume that an ESPP at your new company will be the same as the one at your current company.

Tuition Reimbursement/Assistance. Tuition assistance provides employees with reimbursement (more common) or payment (less common) for education costs. Most employers require the degree or classes to relate to the employee's current job or one they might foreseeably move into with that employer. Policies vary, but many organizations only reimburse expenses up to an amount that's tax-deductible for them.

Student Loan Repayment. This is a new benefit that a handful of employers are using to attract recent college graduates. Companies pay a fixed amount per month or per year to help offset student loan debt.

Discount Programs (company product or other). Many companies that make products or deliver services to their customers offer employees company discounts. When these are significant, employers make a big deal of them in their offer letters (as they should!).

Large companies also frequently offer discounts for gym memberships and other products and services. While there's nothing for you to negotiate here, it's definitely a great thing to investigate after you start working for a new company.

Recognition Programs. Recognition programs are designed for employees to recognize (and sometimes, reward) their peers or for managers to recognize (and sometimes, reward) their employees for doing awesome work. This will likely be something you don't hear about until you're working at a company, but it's a great indicator of how the culture comes to life.

Remote Work Benefits. If your job has a substantial remote work component, it's great to check on benefits relating to that. Does the company cover the cost of teleconferencing services? How about upgraded monitors, video cameras, or phones? Do they have an office furniture allowance? There isn't a true market standard for these benefits, so it's important to ask.

Pet Benefits. Some companies allow pets to come to work with you, and some offer pet healthcare insurance. These are becoming more common, so if they're important, ask!

PRO TIPS

- Most companies offer health and dental insurance. Know what's covered as well as what your premiums (how much you pay every month) are.
- Retirement programs, including 401(k) matches, can vary widely between companies.
- Paid time off programs can be quite different from one place to another, too.
- Differing costs and levels of benefits can have a big impact on your total rewards, especially below the executive level.

Relocation

Relocation benefits are designed to help you and your family move to a new location for work. Please know that relocation services differ widely from company to company, so the list below is likely to include things you won't get in your package, and it will likely *not* include some of the stuff you'll actually see in yours.

Also know that relocation services are almost always tied to the level of the job. A recent college graduate might only receive a small allowance for moving their household goods, where a C-suite executive for a large, multinational company would likely be offered a comprehensive relocation package. Again, it all depends on the company and the job.

What we're talking about here is moving across the country. If you're looking at an international move, it's a whole different — and more complex — ball game, so don't depend on this list to guide you.

RELOCATION BENEFITS

Origination Services. These are benefits that apply to the location you're moving *from*. Things like the cost of breaking your current lease or reimbursement of service termination (like internet service) would be included here.

Household Goods Move. This is moving your stuff (furniture, clothes, cars, etc.) from one place to another. A company could offer to pay mileage for popping your stuff in your car and driving it to the new location, or they could pony up for a moving van with people to pack up your stuff, move it, and unpack it at your destination. Insurance for your household goods is included with moving services, so for those of you who are uneasy about packing services, that can help you feel more comfortable.

Home-Finding Assistance. Your potential company could offer you a visit to the new location to look at houses or apartments, and they might pair you up with a realtor in the new destination to help you find your new place. Most companies offer a single home-finding trip, but a few offer more at higher levels.

Transportation. This is how you'll get from your origination location to your destination. The company could specify anything from expecting you to drive your own car (and typically paying you a per-mile reimbursement) to flying you to the new destination.

Relocation services are almost always tied to the **level of the job.**

Most relocation policies specify whether they expect you to drive your car or ship it to the new location based on the distance between your current location and your new one. The policy may have different practices depending on distance between your old and new locations.

For instance, the company may ask you to drive your car to the new location if it's less than 400 miles away, but they would pay for transporting the car if you're farther away than that.

Destination Services. Destination services includes everything from temporary housing and a rental car in the new location while you wait for your household goods to arrive, to assistance in purchasing a new house or renting an apartment, to helping your spouse find a new job.

Home-Selling and/or Home-Buying Assistance. These benefits are not hugely common, and they're typically limited to people at more senior levels in the company who are current homeowners. Assistance services can vary widely, too, and may include things like realtor or assessor fees, closing costs, and even points on your mortgage. When you're offered these services, you'll likely be required to use company-specified vendors.

Relocation Allowances. Some companies offer a relocation allowance instead of specified benefits, especially for recent college graduates. This allowance comes in the form of a lump sum that's generally paid out after you start your new job.

Be sure to ask whether the bonus is "grossed up"— that means that the bonus will be what you get *after* taxes are taken out. A "$5,000 bonus, grossed up" means that you'll see the full $5,000 in your bank account; a "$5,000 bonus" typically means that you'll have significantly less in your check after the taxes are taken out. Most companies don't gross up bonuses, but you can always try negotiating a higher bonus to offset the taxes.

It's also becoming more common for companies to offer some sort of allowance for relocation, even if the company provides a comprehensive moving package. These allowances are meant to cover anything from costs to set up new utilities, to licensing your cars, bikes, or pets, to...well, whatever you need. Companies offer these allowances not only to make things easier when you're moving, but also to avoid dickering with employees about every little cost and reimbursement. Smart!

Timing. If you have school-aged kids and your company asks you to move in the middle of a school year, you may be able to negotiate a solution that allows your kids to complete the semester (or school year, for older children).

If the company doesn't have a standard way to handle these situations, you could propose extending temporary housing in the new location for yourself between the time you start your new assignment and when the rest of the family moves. Or you might be able to negotiate staying in your home location, with more extensive business travel to the new office until the end of the academic period.

PRO TIPS

- Relocation services can vary a lot and are typically tied to the level of the job.
- International moves are very different than moves within a country.
- If a job change requires you to move and the company doesn't provide relocation benefits, try to negotiate a relocation allowance to help cover your costs.

Other Stuff

People don't typically think much about the "Other Stuff" in this section when they're negotiating their pay packages, but they should. Some of the items listed here can have a profound impact on how much you love your job as well as how your work interfaces with the rest of your life.

Much like benefits, these things aren't typically negotiated. That said, you definitely want to know what the work conditions and intangibles of the job look like before you accept a job because they can have big effects on your day-to-day work life.

WORK CONDITIONS

Work Schedules. It's important to know how much people work and when they do it. Some employers expect you to be in the office from 7:30 a.m. to 5:30 p.m. and to be available for conference calls before and after that. Others have flexible start and end times. Some need employees to be available in the evening or on the weekends, either with or without corresponding time off. This is an area that has a huge impact on your quality of life, and most people don't even ask about it until after they start a job!

Location. Where you live and work can be a big factor in how happy you are. If you love big city life, and you're working and living in a rural location (or vice versa), that can be a bummer. When you're part of a close-knit family, being close enough to see them regularly can be a huge plus. You may choose to live in a less-than-ideal location for a period of time, too, in order to have a particular career experience. It's important to go into things with your eyes open, regardless of your choice.

Commute. Having experienced commutes ranging from zero (working from home) to 90 minutes each way, it's no surprise that commute time has had a major impact on my own life, and I'll bet it will on yours, too. If you have a long commute, but you're able to shift your work schedule, work remotely part of the time, or use public transportation, that can be of great help here.

The 'other stuff' part of your rewards may not be negotiable, but they can have profound impacts on **how much you love your job.**

Office Space. Where will you be working? How does this mesh with your natural work style? Will you have the opportunity to work remotely? This is another area that folks tend not to look into before joining an organization. But they should.

Responsibilities. Getting clear on exactly what you'll be doing on a daily basis is really important! Sure, you can look at the job description, and you can ask your potential manager, but talking with peers could give you a great perspective on things, too. Put this into the category of things you need to know before accepting the offer but won't necessarily be able to negotiate.

Growth Opportunities. If there are ample opportunities to learn and grow, both in the role you're looking at right now, as well as beyond it, that could make your offer even more attractive.

Start Date. This is the date you start working at your new company. I always recommend taking a minimum of a week between jobs, and more (up to four weeks) if you can swing it financially. Taking some time to recharge and to handle personal items can make a real difference in how you show up to your first day in your new job.

INTANGIBLES

Organization and Team Culture. This is another thing that's super-important to get as much information about as possible *before* you start work. You'll get some hints through how the organization talks about benefits and work schedules, but do ask some pointed questions about

culture so you know what you're getting yourself into.

Brand Recognition. This may or may not be important to you. It's fun (trust me!) to work with a consumer brand that has a great reputation. And it can be frustrating to explain over and over what exactly it is that your company does. By the same token, some of my best work experiences have been with places nobody's ever heard of.

DE&I. Diversity, equity, and inclusion can come to life in an organization in different ways, but the best companies actively incorporate DE&I into their culture at all levels in the company.

Direct Manager. It's so awesome to have a great boss! And yes, this could be a key element of the job offer for you.

A word of caution, though. While you always want to feel great about the person you report to, your relationship with your manager can't be the only thing drawing you to a job. Because people change roles and jobs, make sure the rest of the package — both tangible and intangible — makes sense for you.

Organization Leadership. While organization leadership can change over time, too, it's great to scope out who's at the top of the company before you join. What kind of experience and backgrounds do the senior leadership teams have? Is the board of directors made up of people you respect? I like to see diversity in the leadership of organizations I work with — different backgrounds and lived experiences can make for better innovation and growth over the long term.

PRO TIPS

- Work conditions and intangibles are rarely able to be negotiated but important nonetheless.
- One of the things you can — and should — negotiate is a break before you start your new job, if possible.
- Weigh the intangibles, like culture and leadership, as you're evaluating your offer.

Chapter 3

Cost of Living vs. Cost of Labor

The cost of living vs. cost of labor concept is so important, I'm dedicating an entire chapter to it. They're different — but related — concepts, and you need to know how each of them can impact your pay.

COST OF LIVING

Cost of living, from a compensation perspective, is a comparison of a set basket of goods (housing, groceries, utilities, etc.) across different locations. These numbers, expressed as a percentage of national average, can give you a good sense for how much it costs to live in one location versus another.

For example, in the U.S., the cost of living in New York City is far higher than the cost of living in rural Texas. In New York the same basket of goods costs more than twice the national average, and Harlingen, Texas clocks in at a super-low 75% of national average. For reference, the cost of living in Atlanta, Pittsburgh, and Dallas is close to the national average. (And p.s., most people live in places that are somewhat close to the national average cost of living.)

Please note: cost of living is *not* the same thing as **what jobs are paid** from one location to another. For that, we have...

COST OF LABOR

The cost of labor refers to how much organizations pay for a particular job in a particular location. Like our example above, companies do pay more for labor in cities like New York and San Francisco and less in places like rural Texas. However, the differences aren't always proportional to the cost of living (especially at the high and low end), and cost of labor doesn't always correlate with cost of living.

In general, jobs in the highest cost of labor areas (like New York and San Francisco) can pay upwards of 20% more than the national average, while the lowest cost of labor areas tend to pay closer to 10% less than national average. Geographic pay differences can vary by job, industry, location within the metro area, and lots of other things, so please take this as a directional concept instead of an actual number.

As a general rule, you'll see more of a pay differential at lower levels in the organization, because companies recruit locally for those jobs. On the other hand, companies tend to recruit more regionally and nationally for mid- and top-level jobs, and they're paid more alike from one city to another.

COMBINING COST OF LIVING AND COST OF LABOR

When you put cost of living and cost of labor together, sometimes, you see weird things.

For instance, Portland, Oregon and San Diego, California both have similar costs of *labor* (a bit above national average). But the cost of *living* in San Diego is much higher than it is in Portland, so things will cost more in San Diego, as a whole. Although the weather in San Diego is way nicer (sorry, Portland!), so that could help make up for the difference intrinsically, even if you wouldn't see it in your wallet.

In places like Harlingen, Texas, pay will likely be lower than national average, and cost of living will be far lower than national average. In places where the cost of living is far lower than the average cost of labor, expect your dollar to go a lot farther than it might go elsewhere.

In New York or San Francisco, pay will likely be significantly higher than the national average; however, the dramatically higher cost of living will more than offset the higher salary. Of course, there are amazing benefits to working and living in these fantastic cities (just ask the millions of people who do!) that can make it worth the tradeoff.

Given the cost of living and cost of labor, why wouldn't everyone want to work and live in Harlingen? Why would anyone want to work and live in San Francisco? Clearly the equation for quality of life includes more than these two factors. Only you can decide what's right for you.

How much it costs to live in a place and how much employers pay there will impact both **your pay and your standard of living.**

REMOTE WORK

When you're hired as a remote worker (you typically work from home and don't go into a company-owned office), be sure to get clear on what "remote" really means. Will the company expect you to be in the office or travel occasionally? Will you be expected to work specific hours of the day or week? It's important to start with a shared understanding of the company's expectations.

With remote work, there are three basic ways a company can handle setting your pay rate:

1. Based on the *company's* home location.
2. Based on the *employee's* home location.
3. Based on *national market* conditions.

These three methodologies can bring different results for you, depending on your location and the company's location, especially if you live in a place that's not near the national averages for cost of living and cost of labor.

If you're being hired for remote work, chances are good that your recruiter (or offer letter) will talk about what they're basing pay on, but if they don't, it's totally cool to ask. And it's especially important to know if you're planning to move at any point during your tenure.

PRO TIPS

- Cost of living is how much it costs to live in a place; cost of labor is how much organizations pay for talent. They're not the same thing.
- When you're moving, you need to understand both the cost of living and the cost of labor to help you understand the impact to your quality of life.
- Companies have different ways to calculate pay for remote workers. You should know how this works, just in case you decide to move somewhere else down the line.

Chapter 4

What Can (and *Can't*) You Negotiate?

Let me start out by saying that you can try to negotiate anything. Don't run around saying that I told you that you could only negotiate certain things. Because I'm not saying that.

What I am saying is that certain things are more commonly negotiated than others, and depending on the organization and situation, going after the uncommon ones may feel like you're banging your head against the wall. I'll explain why in a sec. But bottom line: you do you.

Some things just can't be negotiated, and that's not personal.

Especially in larger companies, salary and benefits elements can be policy-driven. This can include who's covered with certain benefits, bonus percentages, 401(k) contribution, stock treatment, and stuff like that. Making exceptions to some policies can put the benefit plan itself at risk with government regulators, so that may be a reason you're not able to negotiate on specific things.

Some companies are simply more flexible than others when it comes to pay, too. Smaller organizations can often have flexibility with the mix of elements in the pay package, trading more of one thing for less of another. But larger organizations often have more and different pay and benefits along with less flexibility about mixing.

There will also be things at play internally that you don't/can't/won't have access to information about.

Internal equity (how people are paid relative to each other inside the organization) can often be a factor.

If your salary requirements are higher than others doing the same job, that can be tough for the company to accommodate. If they're higher than your new boss' pay, it can be a deal-breaker. And that's not saying you're wrong about what you're asking for, but it can make things a mismatch between you and the company.

Know, too, that with equal pay coming to the forefront, there may not be much wiggle room with starting rates, either. But that shouldn't stand in the way of asking for what you want, because...lots of stuff *can* be negotiated.

MOST COMMONLY NEGOTIATED ASPECTS OF YOUR OFFER

Base Pay. This is the big dog of the negotiation game. In fact, some people think this is the only one that matters (which may be true for you...or not). Recruiters and hiring managers expect some negotiation here, so there's no reason *not* to try.

Sign-on Bonus. Because sign-on bonuses are meant to sweeten the offer and help tip the balance in the company's favor, *and* because they're a one-time cost to the company, candidates frequently negotiate them.

Sign-on Equity. There are two different types of sign-on equity negotiations — equity for startups, and equity for more mature companies. Because they're fundamentally different, you negotiate them a bit differently, too.

- *Startup sign-on equity*. Equity for startup companies tends to be the lion's share of the equity you'll get (some startups offer refresh grants, too, but they tend to be much smaller when offered). Because this is such an important part of the package for startups, and because it has long-term ramifications for your pay, I always recommend that my clients who go to startups work on negotiating this piece.
- *More mature company equity*. Equity for companies other than startups tends to be negotiated much like sign-on bonuses. Because sign-on equity at mature companies won't likely have a major impact on future annual grants, there's not as much pressure to negotiate this at the time of your offer.

Timing of Next Pay Review. I advise clients who haven't been able to negotiate higher base pay (there are lots of reasons this might happen) to request an earlier review of their pay than they'd typically be eligible for. After a period of 6 months (or even 3), you'll be in a better position to show the value you're actually adding in the organization, and may make an even more compelling case for a raise.

Paid Time Off. While vacation and paid time off tends to be a policy thing in most organizations, you may be able to negotiate the time off you get, especially in your first year. If you have vacation or wedding or holiday plans already in place when you get your offer, you can frequently negotiate getting some additional time off, which might be paid or not.

Relocation Benefits. Like sign-on bonuses, relocation benefits are one-time costs to the company. And relocation policies are designed to fit most cases — not all. If you need an extra week of temporary housing before moving into your new digs or some extra bucks to help you move your Great Dane, check to see how your company could accommodate you. Again, it's not always going to work, but it doesn't hurt to ask!

Work Schedules. Companies are getting more and more comfortable with remote work and alternative work schedules. If this is important to you, ask to see how close you can come to your ideal situation.

Start Date. While some jobs and some employers require specific start dates (this is more likely if you're joining a rotation program or something like that), most places are happy to accommodate your need to adjust your start date, by a couple of weeks, at least.

ITEMS YOU MAY HAVE TROUBLE NEGOTIATING

Benefits. Most companies have a benefits policy that's the same for all employees, so trying to get a lower premium or higher benefits might not be your best shot at getting a better offer.

Relocation Benefits. Yup, you read it right. This one shows up in both "commonly negotiated" AND "you may have trouble" sections. That's because you might be able to negotiate some elements but not others. Here's why. Relocation policies tend to be the same by level in the organization (for example, recent college grads might get a small allowance, and EVPs might get a package that includes costs of both selling and buying a home).

Some things **can't** be negotiated, and that's not personal.

While it might be relatively easy to negotiate something that's within your current level, it may be tough to negotiate something that's only offered at a higher job level. You probably won't know if what you're asking is within your level or not unless you ask and get denied.

Paid Time Off. Like relocation benefits, paid time off/vacation tends to be policy-driven in most companies. If you really cannot abide the company's PTO policy, you can ask about negotiating extra time off without pay (and consider negotiating a higher base pay to make up for it).

Stuff about the Job. The responsibilities of the job, including where it reports and which jobs report to it, can be hard to negotiate as a candidate. The more senior the job, though, the more likely this will be discussed in the interview process.

Stuff about the Company. You're not going to be able to influence the culture or leadership of the company as a candidate. Unless you're Beyoncé. She can do anything.

PRO TIPS

- You can try to negotiate anything.
- Some things are easier or more typical to negotiate than others.
- Base pay and start dates are the most commonly negotiated items.
- Things that are dictated by policy (like paid time off) or by level (like bonus percentages) may be difficult to negotiate, and it's not personal.

Chapter 5

Toolset Client Story

A couple of things to note, since this is our first client story. I work with clients at all levels in their organizations. And while it's important for you to see how the things I'm teaching come to life for actual clients, I don't share any identifying information to ensure their privacy and confidentiality.

Know that the stories I'm telling here are real client experiences negotiating pay in different industries and different types and levels of jobs. I want you to see how the information in this book can take shape in different ways.

To illustrate the power of your Toolset, I want to share a story about a salary negotiation client of mine. This client was moving from a management role in a consulting practice to an executive role in a small, for-profit company.

They weren't sure what the best source of market data for positions like theirs would be. Fortunately, the data we were looking for was publicly available in the proxy statements for publicly-traded companies. We looked at base pay, bonus targets, equity, and employment agreement terms for jobs like theirs in companies similar to the one they expected to get an offer from.

My client then made a detailed list of the considerable value and unique skills and talents they would bring to the prospective company. (This was a fantastic Mindset and confidence booster!)

Armed with this information, they were able to decide exactly what they wanted to target for base pay, bonus, and equity before they even received an offer. When the offer did come in, they were able to quickly consider it, and confidently negotiate their targets for each pay element.

The results? An 18% increase to the original base pay offer and bonus target amount, plus more favorable terms in their employment agreement. Yes!

Chapter 6

Toolset Q&A

Q: I'm in a really niche type of job. How do I find out what the market is for it?

A: After spending most of my career in corporate compensation, I haven't found tons of jobs that are so unique that market data can't be used to help explain them. Some are, of course, but most jobs share things in common with others. Even in "niche" jobs, it's typical to find about 80% of the job similar to one you'd find in the market, with 20% being more unique or specialized.

The good news about that is that you can find jobs that are largely similar in the marketplace, and then nudge the market data up a smidge to account for any differences. And chat with your professional organization — they may be able to help you narrow in on your target market even better.

Q: What's the best way to ask my friends in other companies what they're getting paid?

A: People can still be a little weird about talking about their pay, even though it's a lot more common than it used to be. You'll often be more successful asking a bit less directly, like asking if the range you're targeting makes sense to them.

Q: What's better to get, stock options or RSUs?

A: It depends (I know, I say that a lot!). It depends on your tolerance for risk, on your view of how the company will grow, and how long you intend to stay at the company.

If you're risk-averse or you're at a company that's more mature in their growth curve, RSUs (Restricted Stock Units) may be more attractive to you. If you're confident about the rapid growth of your company's stock, options may be more to your liking.

That said, most companies offering equity don't allow you to choose which vehicle you prefer. If you do have a choice, please consult your financial advisor to decide what's best for you.

Q: My relocation info says that I can get either a cash allowance to spend any way I want to or I can have a company pack up my stuff and move it. I feel weird about having other people in my house and touching all my things, so I was thinking I'd just take the allowance, instead. Good idea, or no?

A: In most cases, it'll cost you more to cover the expenses of a move than the benefits the company will offer in a relocation package. Look at the policy carefully to see which is the better deal for you. And even if you have movers packing your things, you can still pack any of your most personal items yourself. But remember, your movers will be pros!

Q: Should I accept an offer from a company that only has white guys on their board of directors?

A: That's entirely up to you. In this day and age, there are tons of ways boards can recruit diverse members, and even the most conservative companies are coming to the realization that diverse leadership is more effective. If the leadership of the company doesn't share values with you, it may be challenging to stay aligned with the organization's mission, vision, and culture over the long term.

Q: I'm expecting an offer from a great company in San Francisco. I live in the Midwest, and I have a comfortable salary. When I did the salary comparisons, they showed I should be asking for $200K, which is WAY more than I thought I'd be asking for, but I want to maintain my standard of living. How should I approach this conversation?

A: Congrats! I'll give you a word of caution here... Companies pay based on cost of labor, NOT cost of living. What that means is that they typically target paying the "going rate" for similar jobs in their area.

I'm guessing the $200K figure comes from translating your cost of living in the Midwest to San Francisco, one of the highest cost of living cities in the US, rather than a comparison of the market/labor rates for the same job in San Francisco. While salaries in SF will definitely be higher than what you'd see in the Midwest, they won't be high enough to keep you at the standard of living you're used to.

My best recommendation is to look closely at the market data for the jobs in San Francisco, and think hard about whether or not you could have the life you want there, given their market pay rates. It's perfectly natural for you to want to replace the basket of goods and services on an equal basis, but that's not how things work (speaking from a zillion years in corporate compensation).

That said, ask for what you want, but do it with your eyes open. And if it's a great match, there might be other ways to work things, like remote work or other (less costly) locations.

Q: Can I negotiate everything in the "What's In Total Rewards" section?

A: My philosophy is that you can negotiate anything, but you can't negotiate everything. And some things are easier to negotiate than others. Check out **Chapter 4 | What Can (and Can't) You Negotiate?**.

Q: Why can't I negotiate <fill in the blank with the thing you're most passionate about>?

A: Remember that part where I said "you do you"? That.

Q: What's the weirdest thing you've ever seen negotiated?

A: It's probably something my husband negotiated when we relocated for his work years ago. We have a lovely rocking horse that my dad carved for our daughter. My husband negotiated having the movers build a special crate for moving it across the country so it wouldn't be damaged.

Q: I have no clue what I'm doing, so I figure I'll just go with the offer the company gives me. How wrong could it be?

A: Frankly, if you don't spend any time looking at the market or deciding what it is you want, you may as well accept the first offer you get. But if you're willing to invest some time understanding the market and your offer better, and some additional time figuring out what's important to you, I bet you'll feel a ton more confident entering into negotiations with your prospective employer. And you'll have set yourself up for success, too.

Q: If I leave my current company right now, I'll be leaving tons of money on the table. How do I negotiate that into my offer?

A: If your bonus payout and/or equity vest dates are coming up soon (say, within a month or two), talk with your potential employer about the possibility of moving your start date out. If they're not able to, or if your vest date/bonus date is farther out, see if you can negotiate a sign-on bonus or grant to help make up for the potential value you're leaving behind.

PART 2

SKILLSET

Now, let's talk about your skillset. This area focuses on the skills you need to negotiate your pay well, like assessing your offer, understanding what you're walking away from in your current company, the basics of negotiating, and what (and what NOT) to say.

What's in this section…

Chapter 7: Understanding Your Offer

How to objectively look at your offer. Interpreting information about short-term incentives, long-term incentives, sign-on amounts, and payback policies. How to keep things straight when you have multiple offers.

Chapter 8: Evaluating Your Offer

The role of a gut check in salary negotiations. Comparing your offer to your current pay package. Assessing the offer to your prioritized list. Comparing multiple offers.

Chapter 9: Your "Walk Away Value"

How to calculate the amount of annual bonus you're walking away from with your current company. When to use "walk away value" in negotiations.

Chapter 10: Negotiation Basics

How to decide what you want from the negotiations. The importance of confidence. Negotiating like you would for a friend. Collaboration, not competition. The order you should negotiate your items. Using the anchoring technique. Avoiding negotiation fatigue. Special strategies for executives. Being prepared to walk away from negotiations.

Chapter 11: What to Say...and What NOT to

My 7 Magic Words for salary negotiations. Navigating the salary history and pay expectations discussion. Proven phrases to use in the negotiations. The importance of practice. Why you should never accept on the spot.

Chapter 12: Just Don't

Don't be clueless. Don't be a jerk. Don't wing it. Don't take things personally. Don't make assumptions. Don't listen to your loved ones. Don't melt down. Don't stay with it if you're not into it.

Chapter 13: Skillset Client Success Story

How a client used their Skillset to negotiate a 17% increase in their offer and avoid a $25,000 mistake.

Chapter 14: Skillset Q&A

Questions I get about things in the Skillset section.

Chapter 7

Understanding Your Offer

It's so easy to get swept away with the emotion of getting an offer. It's so exciting! Hurray! Champagne! And congratulations are in order.

But getting an offer isn't the end of the road; it's really the beginning of the most important part of your negotiating journey. Figuring out if you want to accept the offer…or not. Negotiating…or not.

No matter how excited you are, do NOT accept an offer on the spot. It's so, so easy to get carried away with the thrill of it all, but don't (more on that later). You need time to assess your offer and to negotiate. Ask your contact how long you have to consider the offer. Forty-eight hours is generally considered good offer practice, but if you need more time, let them know.

At this point, it's all about understanding. Try to hold off on evaluating and making judgement calls about your offer until you understand all of its component parts. (The judge-y part comes in the next chapter.)

GENERAL GUIDANCE

The first step in any pay negotiation is to understand your offer. What elements are in there? What base pay are they offering? Do you have a bonus? What do the benefits look like? If you're moving to take the job, what does the relocation assistance look like?

Don't just think about base salary. Short-term incentives (like bonuses and commissions), long-term incentives (like equity), benefits (like healthcare, retirement, and vacation), and the culture of the company, are all important. And if there's something in the offer that you're not familiar with, refer to **Chapter 2 | What's in Total Rewards?** for explanations of the most common elements.

Read every single thing that comes with your offer letter (if you have one). All the benefits information, all the relocation information, and everything in the letter itself.

It's crucial for you to spend time with your offer to understand everything that you can.

You. Must. Understand. What. You're. Signing. Up. For.

Besides, you'll be better positioned to ask smart questions and not waste time (or negotiating energy) on things you already have answers to. The questions you ask should not be easily answered by reading things you already have.

That said, if the stuff in your offer package doesn't make sense, you absolutely owe it to yourself to ask enough questions so that you do understand things. And frankly, your prospective employer wants you to understand — and appreciate — every single thing they put in the package!

I'm offering a bunch of clarifying questions for each chunk of pay elements here, but please know that you should be able to answer many of them from the information that's provided to you in your offer packet. Of course, the answers to some of them might not be all that important to you. But if they are, *get the answers!*

BASE PAY

Base pay is usually presented in a pretty straightforward way, but since it's such a big part of the pie, it's super-important you know what things mean.

Exempt Jobs. Most jobs that are exempt (from the Fair Labor Standards Act, so they don't require overtime pay) have base pay expressed as an annual or monthly amount in the offer letter. Every once in a while, an employer will talk about it as "semi-monthly" (twice a month, so 24 pay periods) or "bi-weekly" (every two weeks, so 26 pay periods). Do your math so you know what you'll be getting!

Non-exempt Jobs. Non-exempt (overtime eligible) job offers are typically communicated as hourly rates (multiply by 2,080 for a full-time annualized number). If you're working a different shift than the standard 8 to 5 Monday through Friday, make sure you know whether the amount that's in your offer includes any shift differentials.

BONUSES, COMMISSIONS, AND OTHER SHORT-TERM INCENTIVES

If you want to understand short-term incentives better, there's a whole host of things you need to know.

Past Performance. I encourage all of my clients to ask prospective employers about how bonuses have paid out for the prior three to five years. While past performance doesn't guarantee future performance, it can at least give you some sort of hint as to what the company has been accustomed to, performance-wise.

Timing. The timing of your next bonus payout is important, not just for context-setting, but also as a lever to help negotiate a sign-on bonus (or to justify a larger one). The longer the time between your last bonus payout at your previous company and the first at your new one, the bigger your sign-on bonus should be.

Bonus Plan Design. Depending on how much of your pay will be delivered via bonus, you may or may not need to spend a lot of time understanding the design of your bonus plan. At a minimum, everyone who's eligible for a bonus should know what their target is. But unless your bonus target is more than 25% of your base pay, you probably won't want to spend your negotiating capital understanding plan design specifics before you're hired. Other items will likely be more important.

If your target is at that 25% or more level, it's more likely you'll want to spend time to understand the plan design more thoroughly, including what measures are considered for your bonus, and what the performance spread (threshold to excellence) looks like.

Bonus Performance Spread.

- *Target.* First of all, what's your bonus target? This is the annual amount you're slated to receive if your performance is good (your bonus target is generally expressed as a percentage of base pay). If you're eligible for a bonus or commission, this will be specified in your offer letter.
- *Threshold.* Most bonus plans require you to meet a threshold of performance before they pay out. For individual payouts, most companies don't pay bonuses if your performance is poor. For company-based plans, there might not be a payout if performance wasn't at least as good as the prior year.
- *Excellence.* Most bonus plans also have a maximum level of payout, often expressed as a multiplier (like 150%) of target.

Commission Plans. If you're working on commission, you'll want to understand the design of your commission plan thoroughly before you start negotiating your offer. What are the performance measures? Are there commission guarantees as you start out? If so, how long do they last? How frequently do you get payouts? What percentage of sales people achieve target and excellence performance levels?

LONG-TERM INCENTIVES

If you're receiving long-term incentives, chances are good that these will be a significant part of your pay package, so it's important to understand them.

Long-Term Cash. If you're being offered long-term cash, the target will be specified in the offer letter. You'll likely need to ask about when you'll be eligible for your first payout and what the plan measures are. If you won't be eligible for a payout in your first year, you may be able to negotiate an additional sign-on bonus to help make up for the loss of participation in the program, especially if you are eligible for a similar program in your current company.

Stock/Equity. With ongoing stock or equity grants, you'll want to ask about timing of grants, typical size of grants for strong performers at the level you'll be going into the company, and what percentage of people at your level receive awards. Employers are notoriously noncommittal about grant sizes, so don't be worried if they're not ultra-forthcoming about their equity practices. But still ask!

It's crucial for you to spend time with your offer to understand everything in it. You must **understand what you're signing up for.**

And while you're at it, take a look at the company's stock performance over time. Equity for companies in growth mode is far more valuable than it is for companies that are flat or declining. Of course, past performance is no guarantee of future performance — good or bad — but it can be a good indicator.

BENEFITS

Health & Dental Insurance. You'll want to get clear on your healthcare and other insurance benefits. When will coverage begin? What do your premiums (the amount you pay for coverage) cost? Are the costs each month, or each pay period? Are pre-existing conditions covered or not? What out-of-pocket costs are there?

Chances are good that all of these questions will be answered in the materials you get with your offer letter. It may take a while to wade through everything, but it's important you know what you'll be getting.

If you have (or someone in your family has) a particular medical concern, you may need to direct your detailed questions to the benefits department or the insurance carrier directly to get a clear picture of how the plan would work in your situation. Just ask the person you're negotiating with to connect you with someone who can answer specific plan details.

Holidays/Vacation/Sick Time/PTO. Vacation, sick time, and paid time off (PTO) are all great benefits that you'll want to have a good handle on. Which holidays does the organization have off? Which type(s) of time off program does the company have? How many days (or hours) of time off will you get each year? Does it accrue over time, or do you get your full allowance at the beginning of the year? How will you handle time off of work for illness?

If your organization offers unlimited paid time off, how does that come to life for them? How much time off is typical?

Retirement. Most companies have 401(k) plans (or their nonprofit equivalents), but check to be sure what exactly you'll be eligible for. If so, when are you vested in the company-contributed amount? (Note: the amount that *you* contribute won't be subject to vesting.)

Check for pensions here, too — they're rare, but not unheard-of. Does the company match your contributions up to a certain amount?

Are there other programs designed to help you with retirement, like retiree medical (medical insurance coverage after you retire), or profit-sharing plans? If so, how do they work?

SIGN-ON BONUSES AND EQUITY

Sign-on Bonus. You'll want to clarify a few things with your sign-on cash bonus. First of all, is the amount you're talking about "gross" (without taxes taken out) or "net" (the amount you get after taxes are taken out). Most sign-on bonuses will be communicated as gross amounts, by the way, so you'll need to think about how taxes would impact them.

Next, you'll want to know when to expect the amount to be deposited to your account. Many companies will pay it out along with the first paycheck you get.

Sign-on Equity. From a sign-on equity perspective, you'll want to know the size of the equity award, what its vesting schedule is, and when the grant is scheduled to be approved.

If you're going to work for a start-up company, you need to understand what will happen to your equity if the company is sold or acquired or goes public. I cannot stress this enough — *change of control provisions around equity are the single most important thing you need to understand when you go to work for a startup!*

It's far more likely for a company to be sold or acquired than it is to go public, and the treatment for your equity is likely to be different in those cases than it would be for an IPO (Initial Public Offering). Although equity treatment isn't something you'll likely be able to negotiate, you simply must go into your new job with your eyes wide open.

PAYBACK POLICIES

If you've been fortunate enough to receive relocation benefits, a sign-on cash bonus, or some sort of tuition reimbursement or student loan repayment as a part of your offer, you'll want to know if there are any conditions that would require you to pay the bonus back to the company.

Most employers will have some sort of prorated payback plan if you leave in the first year (sometimes, within the first two years). If you leave within the payback term through a layoff, chances are good that your employer will waive your payback requirement. And if they don't, try to negotiate that with them.

MULTIPLE OFFERS

If you're looking at several offers at the same time (lucky you!), you'll probably want to pop all of this info into a spreadsheet so you can see everything side by side. It can be confusing to remember which offer had what feature when you're looking at multiples.

PRO TIPS

- When you get an offer, take a moment (or a few!) to celebrate, and then dig into the work of negotiating.
- In order to negotiate well, you must understand your package.
- Read everything in your offer letter and accompanying documents, and ask questions if you don't understand.
- While amounts may be clearly stated, it's important to get clear on timing and payback policies (if applicable), too.

Chapter 8

Evaluating Your Offer

Now that you really understand your offer, you need to evaluate how it fits with what you care about, how it compares with your current package, and, if you're lucky enough to have multiple offers, how this one stacks up to the others.

DO A GUT CHECK

When you read your offer letter, how did you feel? Excited? Disappointed? Confused? It's important to check in with yourself before moving forward with the assessment.

If you're confused, you can get more information to clear things up. If you're disappointed in the offer but excited about the job, you can negotiate, and potentially move the offer up. If you're thrilled about both the offer and the job, you can still negotiate your offer and maybe have even more to be thrilled about!

On the other hand, if you already know in your heart of hearts that this isn't the job for you, negotiating a better package won't make it so. Pay and benefits can only go so far, and they certainly can't make up for a bad boss, a poor job fit, or a company that you can't respect.

Bottom line: it's okay to walk away from an offer. And by "walk away," I don't mean you should ghost the employer; decline the offer respectfully. If it's not a good match, or if you get a bad feeling about a job or organization, listen to your intuition!

COMPARE IT TO YOUR CURRENT PACKAGE

I always recommend that my clients compare each element in their offer to what they're getting in their current job. Almost everyone compares base pay to base pay, but that doesn't tell the whole story.

List out all of the pay elements from your current job. (Need help? Check out **Chapter 2 | What's in Total Rewards.**) Now, do the same for your offer. How do things compare? Are there significant differences? And if so, are there things in the new package that make up for what you're missing from the old one?

Because every employer pays differently and has different benefits, not every element will match up. And even a much better offer for a bigger job may have some elements that aren't as good as your current employer's. That doesn't mean you should reject the offer. It just means you should keep it in mind as you negotiate.

A client of mine was concerned about higher healthcare premiums (to the tune of about $250/month) with their new offer. While their significant base pay increase more than made up for the higher premiums, they were still able to use the difference as a point of negotiation.

Compare each element in your offer to what you're getting in your current job and to **your prioritized list.**

Don't forget to weigh in on the intangibles. If you can cut a half hour each way out of your commute, that's a significant benefit. Or if your opportunity for development and advancement is better, or you'd be working with a technology or brand that would benefit your career, those should be a part of your decision, too.

COMPARE IT TO YOUR PRIORITIZED LIST

How does your offer compare to your prioritized list? (**Chapter 15 | Getting Clear** will show you how to make one.)

First, find any showstoppers. If there are elements that are below your minimum acceptable levels, by definition, you'll need to negotiate them at least to a level that is acceptable to you, or you should consider walking away from the offer.

If you're interested in the opportunity, I recommend trying to negotiate these "below floor" items — your potential employer won't know they missed the mark unless you tell them. While they might not be able to meet your requirements, rejecting the offer out of hand definitely won't get you what you want.

Go through your entire prioritized list to see which elements line up and which ones don't. Take notes on where you see opportunity for negotiation. It's also important to know where you don't need or want to negotiate.

This is a great time to remember that this whole process isn't personal, and you shouldn't take it personally. More on that later.

VIEW IT SIDE-BY-SIDE WITH OTHER OFFERS

If you're lucky enough to have multiple offers, it's important to look at how all elements of the packages stack up against each other. Base pay numbers never tell the whole story.

One thing you should *not* expect is to get one of the companies to match all of your favorite items that you've cherry-picked from all of your offers. Companies make different investments in total rewards that reflect their histories and culture, so it's unlikely the same things will be available at the same level in every organization you're comparing.

In addition to the compensation and benefits pieces of the offer, you'll want to compare the not-so-obvious things. If the jobs are in different cities, how do the different costs of living in each place impact your offer? If the jobs are in the same town, how would the commutes differ? How do the cultures and leadership compare between the organizations?

Completing this thorough assessment will provide the foundation for your negotiations.

PRO TIPS

- Do a gut check to make sure it still makes sense to pursue the opportunity.
- Comparing your offer to what you currently have will help you see gaps and opportunities, and it will help you be more realistic about your offer.
- Comparing your offer to your prioritized list will help you decide which items to negotiate.
- If you've got multiple offers, look at them all side-by-side and compare all of the pay elements as well as things like commute, culture, and leadership.

Chapter 9

Your "Walk Away Value"

"Walk away value" is a term compensation folks use to talk about the amount of cash and equity a candidate is walking away from when they leave their current job.

These calculations are great for you to have at hand when you're negotiating your offer — they can help you justify asking for additional base, bonus, equity, or sign-on bonus, especially at more senior levels of the organization.

WALK AWAY CASH

Walk away cash generally refers to the bonus opportunity you're leaving on the table. For example, if you leave your company at the end of September, and your bonus year goes from January to December, you're leaving nine months of bonus "earnings" behind.

Make no mistake, your current company doesn't view your bonus as earned unless you're employed when they pay out the bonus (some companies consider the bonus earned if you're there at the end of the performance period). But had you stayed until the bonus paid out, you would have had a reasonable expectation of getting it.

In our example above, I would calculate your bonus walk away value as (9 months/12 months * bonus target = bonus walk away value). So, if your bonus target was $10,000, your walk away value would be 9/12 * $10,000 = $7,500.

Knowing what you're walking away from at your current company can help you justify **asking for more** from your prospective employer.

Again, this is an estimated and fictitious amount. You're not actually entitled to it, it wasn't any sort of guarantee, and your potential employer doesn't owe you this. And you may not be able to convince the person you're negotiating with to give it to you. But calculating your walk away cash is a legitimate way to help with your negotiating — it's a common practice that anchors to real numbers.

WALK AWAY EQUITY

If you're in the enviable position of having lots of equity in your current job, you'll want to understand what you're walking away from to help you with your negotiations. This used to be something that prospective employers would help to calculate, but given some of the rules around equal pay, many are prohibited from doing so.

Just like walk away cash, walk away equity isn't something you're owed. But for people who are moving between jobs that are both eligible for equity, it's more likely to help you get additional sign-on cash or equity in your negotiations.

If your stock is underwater (the grant price is higher than today's price), you won't have any walk away value. But if you're leaving a ton of equity value when you leave your job, it's natural to want your new company to help offset what you're leaving behind.

Calculating the walk away value of your equity is more complex, and I won't detail the calculation here. Essentially, it's today's value of your equity that would vest in the coming year (or two years, if you're close to a vesting date). And even though you may have more than two years of unvested equity, it would be highly unusual for a company to offset more than two years of walk away value.

If you need help calculating the value of walk away equity, a pay negotiation coach should be able to help you.

WHAT TO DO WHEN YOU'RE NOT ACTUALLY WALKING AWAY FROM ANYTHING

There are several scenarios where you might not be walking away from anything material. If you're leaving your job at the end of your performance period, or if you're in your first job, or you have a break in service, you might not have anything material you're walking away from. And that's okay! You can still negotiate with your prospective employer to get a sign-on bonus.

Whatever you do with walk away value, though, don't lie about it. It's a bad way to start your employment relationship.

PRO TIPS

- While "walk away" value isn't money or equity that's earned or owed to you, it can be very helpful in justifying bigger bonuses, higher equity, or sign-on bonus or equity.
- Do use your actual bonus target or equity grants to calculate walk away value.
- Don't lie about what you're leaving on the table.

Chapter 10

Negotiation Basics

What we've done up to this point has been to figure out what's what. Now, let's look at the basics of negotiation, so you know how to approach it.

KNOW WHAT YOU WANT OUT OF THE NEGOTIATION

This is where your preparation comes into play. Be clear and specific about what's important to you, and know that there are certain things that you may want that the organization is unable or unwilling to negotiate.

If the level of incentive pay seems okay to you, but the base pay doesn't meet your expectations, spend your time talking with them about base pay, not about incentives.

And know that, while the cost of healthcare premiums is almost never negotiable, you might be able to negotiate an increase to base pay that can help offset it, if that's something important to you.

Keep in mind that just because you could negotiate something, it doesn't mean you should. Pay particular attention to how the negotiations are progressing, and remember that negotiation fatigue is a thing (see below).

When you approach negotiations as a **collaborative partnership** where the goal is to have both you and the company satisfied with the outcome, you're more likely to **get what you want**.

AIM FOR COLLABORATION, NOT COMPETITION

Lots of folks think that pay negotiation is a zero-sum game slash virtual cage fight where one person wins and the other loses ("There can be only one!"). And you could approach things that way, but I don't recommend it.

In most cases, you'll be negotiating with a recruiter rather than your future manager, so the recruiter effectively becomes your voice to the company in the negotiations. You want that person on your side, advocating for your position, which is much easier to achieve if you're kind and clear and treat them with respect.

Bottom line: when you approach negotiations as a collaborative partnership where the goal is to have both you and the company satisfied with the outcome, you're more likely to get what you want.

GO FROM BIG TO SMALL

When negotiating, start with the big/ongoing stuff first (base pay, bonus, annual paid time off) and move to the less important/one-time things afterward (sign-on bonus, relocation costs, vacation in the first few months).

And when I say "important," I mean important to you and what you stand for. It's cool if you care more about vacation time than base pay, or vice versa, or something else. That said, most negotiations start with base pay, so if it's one of the top three things you want to negotiate, start with that one.

Rank the pieces of the package you want to negotiate from the most important to the least, knowing you might not get through your whole list. And if it's not really important to you, don't try to negotiate it. It's pretty easy to get negotiation fatigue, and from there, it's just a hop, skip, and a jump to being perceived as a jerk.

ANCHORING

The theory of "anchoring" says that the person who comes up with the first number has the power in the negotiation because every number that follows will be considered in relation to that first number. And while I agree with that, up to a point, I'm not a fan of throwing out a gigantic number just because the psychological principle tells us it may be effective.

I believe anchoring only works in salary negotiation when the numbers are somewhat reasonable to the other party. If the candidate throws out a number that's ridiculously high (or low) to the potential employer, the employer may question whether the candidate is the right fit. Same thing goes for the reverse.

Some people don't feel comfortable being the first one to put a number out there. That's okay, too. But be prepared with what you're going to say if they ask about your salary expectations. (There are scripts for this in **Chapter 11 | What to Say**.)

NEGOTIATION FATIGUE

One thing I like to highlight for my clients when we talk about how to negotiate is the concept of "negotiation fatigue." This means that you can negotiate a few things, but you shouldn't negotiate every single thing. Even if you're an attorney (I've witnessed these over-negotiations from the employer side, and they're not pretty).

After the third item you negotiate, start listening very carefully to the person you're negotiating with for cues that you're over-negotiating and they're getting tired of it. While it's highly unlikely that you'd ever have an offer withdrawn for negotiating (I've never seen it happen), you may start to lose the enthusiasm the other party has to champion your cause. It's the law of diminishing returns. Which is why putting your most important items first is so critical.

NEGOTIATE LIKE YOU WOULD FOR A FRIEND

One of the most important pieces of salary negotiation is getting a little emotional distance from the process, which can seem challenging when you think about how important pay is. But it's hard to negotiate well (impossible, really) if you're on an emotional rollercoaster.

A great technique to get some emotional distance is to act like you're negotiating on behalf of a friend. Not a super-close ultra-best friend (you'd likely be pretty emotionally invested there, too), but someone you like and want things to work out well for.

Being prepared and negotiating like you would for a friend should help you negotiate less emotionally. But if things do get emotional and you feel like it's impacting your ability to negotiate, it's okay to take a pause. Ask the person you're negotiating with if you might meet with them again (soon) once you've had some time to consider the discussion.

CONFIDENCE IS KEY

Aim to project calm confidence in the negotiation process. Notice, I didn't say "swaggering cockiness." Again, it's a collaboration, not a competition. You're aiming for kind but firm. That doesn't mean you just roll over and immediately accept whatever the other person is offering; it means that you're kind and polite, and you're clear about what you're asking for (and you don't act like a jerk if the person isn't able to give it to you).

You'll be more confident when you know what's important to you, you understand the offer well, you have a plan for negotiating, and you've practiced what you want to say.

How you conduct yourself in negotiations will be remembered.

BE PREPARED TO WALK AWAY

Ideally, the organization's needs and yours match up well, but sometimes, they just don't. When things don't work out, try not to beat yourself up about it. If you take a job that's not a match, it's likely to mean heartache in the end.

If you feel confident and secure enough to actually be okay if things don't work out with the job offer, it takes the pressure off so you can stay curious during negotiations. When you're not so tied to the outcome, it's much less likely that you'll wind up doing something you regret (like pushing too hard or seeing a match when there really isn't one).

GET HELP

Don't go it alone – this is hard stuff! Make sure you have someone to bounce ideas off of who has your best interest in mind. Having your school's career counselor or a trusted friend or a salary negotiation coach in your corner can help you focus on what's important and show up the way you want to.

SPECIAL STRATEGIES FOR EXECUTIVE NEGOTIATIONS

Act like a leader. Your interviews are your first opportunity to demonstrate your leadership presence; negotiating your offer is your second. You have the chance to make a lasting impression here — will you be collaborative, clear, firm, and nice? Or not?

Your offer may not get rescinded if you're a jerk during the process, but trust me, word will get around. And many of the people you're working with during the offer process will be in a position to smooth your way in the company at some point or another. Wouldn't you rather start off on the right foot?

Get crystal clear about long-term incentives. This is the area I tend to spend the most time helping my executive clients navigate.

As an executive, chances are pretty good that your long-term incentives (whether they're cash, stock, or a combination of the two) are the biggest part of your pay package. You simply must be clear about how much your long-term incentives are worth, how long they take to vest and what happens to them if the company is bought or sold – or, heaven forbid, goes under.

If you're going to work for a start-up, this piece is even more important, since you're likely giving up some of the base and annual bonus you'd get at a publicly traded company for equity.

Pay attention to the terms of your employment agreement. This one's big, too. If you have an employment agreement, which is not uncommon for C-suite executives, it's important to understand all of the terms therein (as they say).

Sure, it can be confusing, and you might never trigger the terms of the agreement. But you need to pay attention to what happens to your pay if you leave the company, whether it's your idea or the company's.

The top three things my executive clients ask me about are:

- *Change of control agreements* (what happens with your pay when the company changes hands)
- *Non-compete clauses* (what company information you're barred from sharing and which companies you're *not* allowed to work for in the future, and for how long)
- *Definition of termination for cause* (how the company decides if you're leaving the company voluntarily or involuntarily)

Some of these agreement terms can be negotiated, and many cannot, but it's important that you go into your new job with a clear understanding, regardless.

Know how to justify your sign-on bonus or equity. Most of my pay negotiation clients have no idea what to ask for as a sign-on bonus before we start working together. But just because sign-on bonuses (or equity) are discretionary doesn't mean that they're arbitrary.

Most companies use sign-ons to compensate executives for bonuses and/or equity value that they're leaving on the table at the organization they're exiting. When you truly understand the worth of what you're leaving behind, you can have a meaningful conversation with the company about what you're aiming to get.

Don't sweat the details of your relocation package. Yes, relocation is important. You're uprooting your family and changing cities (or even states or countries). But unless you're looking at an international assignment, relocation benefits are relatively small in relation to your overall pay package. And they're one-time costs. Feel free to negotiate here, but remember the risk of negotiation fatigue; you might want to prioritize other, more valuable elements ahead of relocation.

Negotiate the small stuff with a light touch. Just like relocation, when you're at the executive level, letting benefits details derail your negotiation conversation is a mistake. If the new company's benefits are worth a couple of thousand dollars less than the ones you currently have, is that enough to change your mind about the opportunity?

It might be, but as an executive, chances are good that benefits are a very small part of your package. And you could probably replace your awesome free gym membership, stock purchase plan, or life insurance benefit fairly easily on the open market. Keep your eyes on the (total rewards) prize.

Know when you need expert help. You're an expert in your field, not in executive compensation. Executive pay packages are complicated. If you want to truly understand the full extent of your package and maximize your effectiveness in negotiation, partner with a professional salary negotiation coach.

PRO TIPS

- Take the time before you start the negotiation process to know what you really want.
- Collaborate with your recruiter or hiring manager during the negotiations rather than compete with them.
- Negotiate as if you were doing it for a friend — it'll give you a little emotional distance.
- Don't try to negotiate every single thing; negotiate from big to small, and if it's not really important, let it go.
- Be prepared to walk away if the company can't meet what's minimally acceptable to you.
- If you're an executive, show your leadership presence in your negotiations.

Chapter 11

What to Say...and What *NOT* to!

Let's talk about what to say and even more importantly, what NOT to say. I'll cover lots of topics here, but this list won't give you a script for every single scenario.

Check out the Q&As at the end of each section of the book for even more ideas.

But before we get started with scenarios you may face, let me introduce you to my 7 Magic Words.

THE 7 MAGIC WORDS

Salary negotiations can be tricky, especially if you're doing it for the first time. My 7 Magic Words are kind of the training-wheels version of negotiation, and if you can't bring yourself to do anything else, memorize this:

"What kind of flexibility do you have?"

The structure of this question is super-important. It's not: "Do you have flexibility?" (they'll say no). It's not: "I'm wondering what kind of flexibility you have," (that's not a question, and it's more passive). It's: *"What kind of flexibility do you have?"*

Not, "Are you willing to negotiate?" or anything like that. Just the seven words. Even if you're already okay with the offer. Even if you hate the idea of negotiating.

Practice them — you can use them at any stage of negotiating.

WHEN THEY ASK YOU ABOUT YOUR PAY HISTORY OR EXPECTATIONS

Early on in the interview process (and maybe even before your first interview), you may be asked some questions about pay. While it's not exactly part of the negotiation process, it does set the stage for your later talks, so I want you to do a great job here.

Salary History. If you get asked, "What is your salary history?" or "What were you paid in your last job?" or anything like that, don't answer. Or at least don't answer that particular question. Many states are making it illegal for employers to ask you what you're currently making. That's because basing an offer on historical pay tends to disadvantage women and people of color.

And even if it is legal to ask in your state, there are lots of ways to dodge the question (if it's on an application, just write in "Negotiable" in the space).

A better way to approach it is to focus on what you are willing to share — your target pay. "Given what I know about the role so far, I'm targeting the <low-, mid-, or high-> $XXs for base pay."

What *not* to say? Your actual salary history. Or anything that sounds shocked, offended, or whiny.

Salary Expectations. When a recruiter asks you what your pay expectations are, I recommend an assertive approach, like the "I'm targeting..." one detailed above.

If you're worried about being first to say your salary expectations, here's how I coach my clients to answer:

> "Without knowing more about both the role and your pay packages, it's tough to give you a good number here. What is the hiring range for the job so I can be sure we're in the same ballpark?"

Remember, the talent acquisition person or manager you're negotiating with wants to make sure you're in the same universe with pay. They're not trying to lowball you or trick you.

What *not* to say? "I haven't really given it any thought." Or, "I'd rather not say." You don't want to make this a game of chicken, and it really is legit for a recruiter to want to know your expectations are reasonable, given their budget.

If you are bound and determined not to answer the expectations question head on, here's a way you could approach it:

> "This sounds like it could be a great fit for us both. I'd hate for pay to get in the way of that. Can I give you a number when I understand more about the role and the rest of the compensation package?"

USING YOUR GAME PLAN

After you create your game plan (see **Chapter 20 | Creating Your Game Plan**), you can put it to work with some great ways to approach the conversation.

Asking questions. You're likely to have some questions (and the person you're negotiating with will expect that). Make sure they're questions that aren't easily answered with information you already have in the offer letter or the other items included. When you show that you've done your homework, you'll have an easier time getting the questions you do have answered. For example:

- "I noticed that the benefits materials say that this role is eligible for a 20% bonus. When in the year are bonuses paid out?"
- "When I read through the relocation policy, I see that a house-hunting trip is included. Does that trip include my family, or is that just for me?"
- "I was excited to see that sign-on stock options are included in the offer. Could you tell me when the grant date will be?"
- "One of my family members has a health concern, and it's important that I understand how

your health insurance deals with that. Could you put me in touch with someone who could help me with that?"

- "In my interview with the supervisor, they told me that there were openings on all three shifts. Could you help me understand the hours and shift differentials that correspond to each of them so I can make an informed decision?"

Discussing changes you'd like to see. This is the part of negotiations that most people have a tough time with. Remember, you'll want to show up as confident, firm, and kind. Do not be a jerk. This is the place where being a jerk will hurt you most!

Base pay. Some phrases you can use to negotiate base pay include:

- "My research shows that similar roles in this area are paid between $X and $Y..." This shows that you've actually looked at the market.
- "Based on my experience and skills, I'm targeting a base pay of $Z. How close can we get to that?" Again, it's a way to tell them you're familiar with the market. Using "we" in the second part of the statement positions you and the person you're negotiating with as a team solving a problem together. Which you are!
- "What kind of flexibility do you have?" Yep! It's the 7 Magic Words.

You're positioning yourself as positive, proactive, and resourceful.

Other compensation & benefits elements. Phrases to use with other elements include:

- "My current company offers four weeks of vacation, and I see that the <company name> package has two. What kind of flexibility do you have to move that to what I have now?"
- "Based on the gaps I'm seeing between what the relocation policy covers and what I'll need to move, it looks like a difference of $XX. Would the company be willing to reimburse me for those additional costs? Or if not, could I get a sign-on bonus to cover them?"
- "When I read through the sales plan, it looks like commissions are capped at $XX. As you know, I'm the top sales rep at my company now, and I earned $YY last year. How much flexibility could we get at the top end for me delivering outstanding results here like I do at in my current role?"
- "My kid will be graduating from high school in a month, and it's a really important time for us to be together as a family. Would I be able to work remotely between now and then, or would the company be able to push my start date out by two weeks?"
- "That won't work for me. What would work is ____." This is pretty direct, but if you're facing something in the negotiation that's way outside your comfort zone, this could be a way to bring things back to center. Don't use this more than once.

Expressing confidence later in negotiations. It's important to keep upbeat and express confidence, especially later in the negotiation process when you're going in for a second round of talks. Here are some phrases you can incorporate:

- "I really want to say 'yes' to this offer, and if we can get to $XX on base pay, I'll be able to."
- "I so appreciate your partnership on this, and I'm confident we'll be able to resolve these last two details."
- "I'd love to be in a position to accept the offer today!" (Use this when you're really close to what you'd like to achieve in the negotiations, and you just need them to say yes to one last thing.)

My **7 Magic Words** for salary negotiation are: ***"What kind of flexibility do you have?"***

Making a plan to follow up. Sometimes, the person you're negotiating with will let you know what the next steps in the negotiation are, without you having to ask. But if they don't volunteer that information, you definitely need to ask for it. Here are a couple of ways to approach it:

- "I really appreciate all of your help with this process! When do you expect to have answers on my requests?"
- "Thanks so much for all your help! What are our next steps?"

You also need to get clear about the timing of your next contact. I recommend that you offer to follow up yourself so the ball is in your court.

- "I'll plan to call you on Thursday to check in and see where we are."
- "If you expect to hear back from leadership by Tuesday, why don't we set a time to check back in on Wednesday to see where things stand? I could meet any time before 11. Would 9:30 work for you?"

Ending the conversation well. Things to say when wrapping up your conversation include:

- "I'd like to be sure all of the things we've agreed to today are included in the offer letter." And then you can run down your list and ask when you can expect to see the updated offer letter.
- "I'm so excited about this opportunity. I really appreciate all your help!" Make sure you end things on an up note!

When you're done negotiating. If you really want to make a great impression with your new employer, show your enthusiasm for your new job. Try asking:

> "Is there anything you recommend I do before I start so I can hit the ground running? And do you mind if I email you with any questions between now and my start date?" This works especially well when talking with the hiring manager, but feel free to use it with recruiters, too.

WHAT *NOT* TO SAY

There are lots of things not to say. Anything that makes it sound like you're entitled, or shows you haven't read the information that was sent to you, or anything that makes you sound like a jerk. There are a couple of other things you should eliminate from negotiation conversations, too.

Wishy-washy Language. Phrases like: "I was hoping for…", "I believe…", "I think…", "I feel…" weaken whatever you say after them. Compare these 2 statements:

A. "I believe that similar roles are paid between $X and $Y in the market" OR
B. "Similar roles are paid between $X and $Y in the market"

See what I mean?

This is an area of opportunity for most folks who have been socialized against speaking up or asking for things. If you can relate, I encourage you to start noticing where and when this wishy-washy language shows up for you, especially in business settings.

Combative language. When you say things like: "take it or leave it" or "you cannot be serious" (looking at you, John McEnroe!), you're taking risks with your negotiation.

Remember, we're all about collaboration to get the best results. Making your negotiation into a competition where they must lose in order for you to win doesn't serve you (even if your Uncle Albert recommends it).

PRACTICE MAKES CONFIDENCE

Practice what you're going to say. Seriously. Negotiation is nerve-racking for even the coolest of cucumbers. If you have a few handy-dandy phrases that you've practiced, it'll be a ton easier to use them in a stressful situation.

I always work with my salary negotiation clients to practice how they're going to ask for what they want. We figure out what the recruiter or hiring manager is likely to ask them or say, and then craft responses, and then do roleplaying. I ask them the questions, and they practice answering them. It makes a huge difference.

If you've got a trusted friend or family member you can practice with, I highly recommend it. But if you're all by your lonesome, it's still a great idea to practice this stuff out loud and not just in your head. You'll be more likely to speak clearly and less likely to trip over your words.

NEVER ACCEPT ON THE SPOT

It's so tempting to accept an offer — or to negotiate it — on the spot. Getting swept away with the delight of getting an offer (or wanting the discomfort of negotiation to be over) is pretty common. Actually, almost universal. But don't do it.

Negotiating your package is a big deal. You owe yourself a little time to think it over, especially away from the emotion of the moment. You need time to read through the details of the offer package, assess it, evaluate it, and figure out your negotiating game plan.

Recruiters would love it if you'd accept your offer on the spot, without negotiation. It's way easier, and then they can move on to the next position they need to fill. But you shouldn't accept on the spot. Not sure how to get that extra time that you need (and deserve)? Start by telling your recruiter or hiring manager how excited you are to receive the offer, ask for time, and close — you guessed it — on an up note.

When you need more time to decide (because you almost always will), try these approaches:

- "I'm thrilled to have your offer! This opportunity sounds like such a great fit. I'll need some time to review the offer letter and information about your compensation and benefits package. I'd like to have the weekend to put some questions together. When would it be convenient to talk? Thank you so much, and I'm looking forward to talking more next week!"
- "I'm excited to have this offer! I'm sure there are questions I'm not thinking of right now. Could I have 24/48 hours to consider everything?" Sure, you're stalling for time, but it's common to have time to reflect on the offer. Hopefully, you won't have to come back with another negotiation request, but you may have some additional questions, and in any case, you've left the door open.

PRO TIPS

- The 7 Magic Words ("What kind of flexibility do you have?") can be used in most negotiating situations.
- There are lots of ways to answer questions about your salary history or pay expectations.
- Don't use wishy-washy or combative language.
- Practice what you're going to say when you address each element you're negotiating so you'll feel — and sound — more confident.
- Never accept an offer on the spot.

Chapter 12
Just Don't

So far, we've been talking about everything you should do. Now, it's time to look at what you absolutely should avoid when you're negotiating pay.

DON'T BE A JERK (AKA "PAY NEGOTIATION RULE #1")

This point cannot be overemphasized. Really. Nobody likes working with a jerk, in either the short term or the long term. This is so important, I call it my Rule #1 for pay negotiations.

If you're working with an internal recruiter or a head-hunter (external recruiter), they're trying hard to make a good match between the right candidate and the company. They're not trying to mess with you, pull one over on you, or underpay you.

The organization's job is to get the most out of you at what they think is a fair price for the job they're hiring for. It's not to screw you over. Think about it. They want you to start your new job excited to contribute, not with a chip on your shoulder.

Your job, on the other hand, is to get the most out of the organization for what you'll be doing for them. It's your responsibility to stand up for what you want (and to know very clearly what that is). It's okay to be firm, and it's really okay to negotiate (or I wouldn't have written this book). Do remember, though, that you're negotiating with another person and that being polite will never be a wrong choice.

How you conduct yourself in pay negotiations will almost certainly get back to your new manager if you're not already dealing with that person. Don't say or do anything during negotiations that you wouldn't say or do in front of your manager. Polite yet firm wins the day.

DON'T BE CLUELESS

I'm betting that won't be a problem for you, since you're taking steps to prepare by reading this book, but help yourself out here. Read everything in your offer letter package. Understand the pay and benefits practices at your current company and compare them to what's being offered. Know yourself and what's important to you.

There are enough unknowns in the process as it is — you shouldn't add to them because you're too lazy or scattered to check out the information you have access to.

DON'T WING IT

Negotiating your salary is a serious business that can have major ramifications to your personal bottom line. Just like you wouldn't go into a big presentation without doing your research and practicing (a lot!), you shouldn't go into a pay conversation that way, either.

And that practice thing? Don't skip it. Not even the most experienced negotiators talk about pay packages every day. It's crucial for you to have held the words that you will be using in your mouth. Memorizing the 7 Magic Words so they trip off your tongue is a great first step. Rope in a friend or relative, too, to help you practice what you want to say and how you want to come across.

DON'T TAKE THINGS PERSONALLY

Pay negotiation absolutely feels personal because your pay impacts so many facets of your life, but it's not. How much an organization is willing to pay says a whole lot more about the value of the job to the organization than about what you're worth, personally.

Let me say that again. *How much an organization is willing to pay says more about the value of the job to the organization than about what you're worth as a person.*

I was talking with a woman recently who was telling me that she had multiple job offers (yay!), but they had wildly different starting salaries. She wondered why some places valued her more than others.

After getting more details, it sounded like the different companies wanted to hire her for different levels of jobs. They all valued her and her experience (enough to offer her a job!), but each organization valued the job they wanted her to do very differently. That's an important distinction.

Companies are kind of mercenary (and you should be, too). Bottom line, the company's job is to get the best talent (that's you!) in exchange for a competitive pay package. Your job is to get as much from the company as they're willing to give in exchange for what you'll contribute to them.

Business. Not personal.

Your ability to **stick with the discomfort** inherent in negotiation conversations is **key to your success.**

So again, a bit mercenary, right? But that said, recruiters and headhunters advocate better for people they have a connection with, and nobody likes to deal with jerks. If you can take the emotion out of the negotiation, you can be even more effective.

I recommend you act like you're negotiating on behalf of someone you like (a pal or colleague), but don't love (your spouse or your best friend). You want to be interested in the outcome but not devastated if things don't turn out the way you hope.

Because sometimes, they don't.

The answer to the question, "Why can't I get what I want in salary negotiations?" isn't "because you're a bad person" or "because you're not good enough." It's "because it's not a good match." And trust me, that's something that you'd much rather discover before you accept the job.

Sometimes there's no match because you haven't been clear about what it is that you want and what you can offer. More often, though, it's because the employer values the job differently than you do.

If you can remember that hiring managers and talent acquisition experts come to work wanting to do a good job (just like pretty much everybody but narcissists and sociopaths do), it can take a bit of the personal sting out of the match/no match process.

DON'T ASSUME

Don't assume the company will automatically do the "right thing." They might, but then again, they might not. They might not even recognize what the right thing *is* for you at this moment.

Nobody has as much of a vested interest in your pay package as you do. What's right for the organization isn't necessarily right for you, and vice versa. Never give up your negotiating power just to be nice or to avoid a scary or uncomfortable conversation.

DON'T LISTEN TO YOUR LOVED ONES (AT LEAST, NOT TOO MUCH)

Don't depend on your family to coach you on negotiating your salary. Unless you'd pay them for their expertise in the field of pay negotiation, this won't get you the results you're after.

Family and close friends want you to be safe and protected. And they don't want you to be disappointed. Ever. So they might not advise you to take the same risks that an expert would, like asking for more pay, equity, or sign-on bonuses, or negotiating for better employment terms.

That's not to say that these important people in your life don't have a role in your job search and offer journey.

Ask the people you know and trust to let you practice what you're going to say. Ask them to be a sounding board and to help you assess culture and fit. And once you have a negotiated offer, ask them to help you decide whether to accept it. (And if you do have an expert in the family, lucky you!)

DON'T MELT DOWN

I've noticed that there are two main places in negotiations where my clients get a little freaked out. The first happens right before they're scheduled to have their initial negotiation conversation, and the second is when they're waiting to hear back from the company about the results of their negotiations.

This is an absolutely normal and natural thing.

When you get an offer, it's typically after several rounds of interviews, reference checks, and some sort of a background investigation. At this point, part of your brain is screaming, "OMG, I WON!" Which you did! Congratulations!

When you're between that moment of "yay!" and "oh, no — I have to negotiate," it's super-common to want to move on to more of the celebration stuff and run away from the emotionally difficult negotiations in front of you.

But don't do it!

Your ability to stick with the discomfort inherent in negotiation conversations is key to your success. You've got to delay the gratification of relief and celebration — just for a few days — if you want to use your negotiating power well.

I had a client who did a great job in her first negotiating conversations, which happened on a Friday, and she negotiated some significant raises to her total compensation. But she wasn't able to tolerate the discomfort of a second round of negotiations.

She had planned to talk with her future employer about her work conditions (which hadn't yet been discussed), but she would have had to wait all weekend to hear back from her employer. She accepted the offer on Friday instead. Would she have been able to negotiate those items if she'd been able to wait? My guess is that she would have, but we will never know.

By contrast, another client took the perspective that negotiations would be a multi-stage process over several days. She negotiated a great pay package first, and then worked out key items in her employment agreement and relocation services. Her patience and tenacity definitely paid off with higher base, bonus, sign-on, and relocation benefits.

Set realistic expectations for yourself about the negotiating process. It's almost never a one-time conversation that's resolved on the spot with a single conversation. When you're prepared for the emotional tax of these discussions, it's much easier to live with the ambiguity while you're waiting for the final resolution of your offer.

DON'T STAY WITH IT IF YOU'RE NOT INTO IT

Getting an offer and negotiating it well means nothing if you don't really want the job. If you're not serious about it, don't waste your time and that of the company.

And if something during the process tips you off that it's not the right fit (either the job isn't what you're looking for, or you're not comfortable with the organization, or whatever), cut your losses. Don't keep pouring your emotional and mental energy into the process.

You can't make a bad match into a good one with compensation and benefits. If a marginally better rewards package wouldn't shift your perspective from, "I'm not so sure about this..." to, "I'm definitely excited!" that's a great clue that you should thank the hiring manager and recruiter and gracefully bow out.

PRO TIPS

- Don't be a jerk when you're negotiating salary. It won't help you, and chances are very good that it will harm you (maybe even long-term).
- Don't take things personally. It's not personal.
- Don't come to negotiations unprepared. This is too important.
- Be prepared for the mental and emotional burden of negotiations so you don't melt down during the process.
- Don't negotiate an offer you know you're not going to take.

Chapter 13

Skillset Client Success Story

I'd like to highlight how important your negotiating Skillset is with another client story. This client was in the early stages of their career and was excited to have a job offer from their dream company in a different location.

When I met them, there were some things in the offer letter and relocation policy that they didn't understand, and they didn't know what was appropriate to ask for.

They didn't recognize the difference between cost of living and cost of labor, and initially wanted to negotiate a far higher base to make up for the cost of living differences.

The job offer had an equity component, which was something they weren't receiving in their current role, so they downplayed the importance of it in the new one.

In addition, my client had the choice between a cash relocation allowance and paid relocation benefits that were handled by an outside firm. Their first thought was to accept the cash allowance to have more control of spending.

We talked through what to expect from the negotiating process, and I helped them demystify some of the things in the offer letter and practiced what to say so they could negotiate from a place of confidence and get more of what they needed from their new company.

When we discussed cost of living and cost of labor, they revised their base pay expectations (although they still wanted to negotiate base pay). We roleplayed how the conversation might go, and they practiced the phrases they wanted to use.

Once they understood the value of their equity offer, it quickly made it to their list of things to negotiate.

And understanding the relocation policy better helped them confidently select the generous relocation benefits instead of the allowance, which wouldn't have covered nearly as many costs.

Because my client was able to understand and evaluate the rewards they were offered, and had planned and practiced their approach, they were able to negotiate competently and confidently. They avoided a $25,000+ mistake with relocation, plus they increased their initial base, bonus, and equity offer by over 17%.

We were both over the moon with their results!

Chapter 14

Skillset Q&A

Q: I have two offers. How do I pick?

A: That's so awesome! My first recommendation on this one actually has very little to do with salary negotiation. Assuming that the offers are somewhat close, I'd pick the opportunity that looks to have the best fit with your long-term career goals.

If you can't figure that out from what you've discovered during the interview process, you could look at which company has the best growth potential. This is even more important for those in jobs that have equity as a part of their pay.

Q: I got a great offer! Or at least I think it is. How do I know?

A: Remember all that work you did in the Toolset section about understanding the market? Refer to that. It'll help.

If you're curious about whether or not your benefits are up to par, that's a great topic to chat with friends about. People are even more likely to share information about their benefits than they are about pay. If you can talk with someone in the same industry and company size (or even better, the one you've got an offer from), that's even better.

Q: I'm really excited about the offer I got — everything's great except there are no relocation benefits, and I'll be moving across the country for the job. What can I do?

A: I'd recommend trying to negotiate a sign-on bonus to help cover your relocation expenses. Estimate your moving expenses (including the costs for moving your household goods and car if you have one, a house-hunting trip, and temporary housing while you wait for your apartment or house to be ready to move into).

Those costs can be the basis of what you ask for as a sign-on bonus. Check out **Chapter 2 | What's in Total Rewards,** too, to see if there are any things you might not have thought about.

Q: What if I want more than the high end of the range the recruiter has quoted me?

A: It's okay — smart, even — to be up front with your recruiter about your expectations. Make sure those expectations are informed by good market research, though. Talk with the recruiter about the level of the job.

If the employer has slotted the job lower than your expectations, that's a sign it might not be a good match for you. If it looks like a good match, and you're not too far off their hiring range, you may want to keep going with the process to see if you can negotiate to get base pay into your range, or if the other elements of the offer may make up for a base pay that's lower than you'd like.

Q: There's just something that just doesn't feel right about this opportunity. I'm getting conflicting answers about the job and the offer, and it's all weird. What should I do?

A: I recommend a two-part approach. First, get curious. What could be driving the weirdness? Are you hearing one thing from the functional leaders but something different from the recruiter? If so, it's totally fine to ask (respectfully) about the differences.

But if you're still feeling uncomfortable after asking questions, listen to your gut. You're looking at making a long-term decision. If it doesn't feel like the right one, don't jump into it if you don't absolutely need to.

Q: I know I want to negotiate my base pay, my vacation, and a couple of things in my relocation package. What order should I approach things?

A: That depends on what's important to you.

If they're equally important, I'd recommend starting with base pay (it's the most commonly negotiated element), and then vacation, and then relocation (since it's a one-time cost to the company). If the vacation piece is about taking time off in your first year for a vacation that you've already got on the books, I'd probably push that one to last.

Bottom line: prioritize important/ongoing items earlier in your negotiation; less important/one-time things can come later in the conversation.

Q: I hear that the person who asks for the actual amount they want to make always loses. Is this true?

A: Actually, it's closer to the opposite. In negotiation terms, the number that gets spoken first is called an "anchor" because every number after that relates to the first number (either higher or lower). Many negotiation experts advise that you should always be the first to say your number so the negotiation is anchored to it.

I think either way can work well. If you're confident you know the going rate for the job as well as how you should be paid relative to it, go for it! If not, it's absolutely fine to ask the company to go first.

Q: I've heard that unless you really play hardball with a company, you won't get what you want in negotiations. Is that true?

A: Nope. My salary negotiation clients who have done the best in their negotiations have approached them with calm confidence, rather than using a hardcore adversarial stance. This lines up with what my recruiter friends tell me, too.

Q: The recruiter for the job I'm interviewing for says they can't move the base pay any higher than what they've offered. I'm sort of okay with it, and the rest of the package is great. Is there anything I can do to push the salary higher?

A: Maybe. The good news is that you'd be okay if things didn't move from where they are now. That's a great place to negotiate from. You know what? You're never going to be as attractive to a prospective employer as you are when you have an offer, but before you've accepted it.

So make sure they know you're excited about the opportunity, let them know you're targeting a slightly higher base pay, and ask them how close they can get to it. They might not be able to go higher, but then again, they might! And don't overlook other elements of pay. Negotiating a higher bonus or sign-on can be a nice added boost.

Q: I was just offered a job for $5K less than I thought I was going to get, given what we'd discussed during the interviews. How should I approach this conversation?

A: You could say something like this: "Based on what I know now about the role and the rest of the compensation and benefits, I'm targeting $XX for this role. How close can we get to that?"

Q: In my interview, my interviewer asked me what my pay expectations were. I flipped it around and asked him for their hiring range. He told me a minimum that was way below the range I was expecting. Do I need to settle for less than what I think is right?

A: Salary ranges can be quite wide, so it could be totally legit that the range low is way below your low. I wouldn't really get concerned about that piece.

I would, though, listen really hard during the interview process to be sure that you're both aligned on the level of the role and its responsibilities. If you are aligned on the job, and your offer then comes in lower than you'd like, you can always use the trusty phrase, "Based on my research, jobs like this one pay between $XX and $YY in the market. And considering what I know of your compensation and benefits plans, I'm targeting $ZZ. How close can we get to that?" Good luck!

Q: What do I say when a company asks me my pay history?

A: I advise my clients not to answer pay history questions. More and more states and cities are outlawing the practice of requesting pay history. Why? Because it perpetuates lower pay for women and people of color. You can redirect this question by using the approach for talking about your expectations.

Q: I got a great offer from a great company! Can I just accept it without negotiating?

A: Sure! But why not practice your negotiating skills? I'd recommend using the 7 Magic Words to see if there's any room for negotiating base pay, at a minimum.

Q: My friend and I are both looking for jobs, and we want to see who can get the most offers (and, of course, the biggest!). How can I get the edge on them?

A: I love me some friendly competition, but this one is flat out silly. It's not the kind of competition that serves anyone well. Not to mention the fact that it might cost you some reputation points in the long run.

You focus on what's important to you, and let your friend focus on what's important to them. It's not likely to be the same thing. If you know you don't want to take a job, don't pursue it. That wastes your time and that of the company. The world of recruitment is a small one, and if you burn your reputation as a serious candidate with one company, the word might get around.

PART 3

MINDSET

We've talked about:

...Your Toolset: the tools and information you need to make great decisions

...Your Skillset: the skills you need to get it done

Now, let's talk about your Mindset. This section will help you set your intention and get out of your own way.

A lot of people focus on the Toolset and Skillset sections, but to be honest, my clients tell me the biggest game-changer for them is in the Mindset.

What's in this section...

Chapter 15: Getting Clear About What's Important...to YOU

Knowing what's important...to you. Prioritizing total rewards elements. Establishing a minimum acceptable "floor" amount for different aspects of pay. Clarity exercises.

Chapter 16: Mindset Shifts

Rejecting assumptions about you and the person you're negotiating with. Resetting your mindset. Knowing how you want to show up in your negotiations.

Chapter 17: It's NOT Personal

Why the negotiation process — and ultimately, your offer — isn't personal.

Chapter 18: Mindset Client Success Story

How a client shifted their Mindset and negotiated a 56% increase to their sign-on bonus.

Chapter 19: Mindset Q&A

Questions I get about stuff in the Mindset section (and how I answer them).

Chapter 15

Getting Clear About What's Important...to *YOU*

With pay negotiation, you need to get super-clear about what's important to you. Not your friends, your spouse or partner, or what you've heard other people think is important. *You.*

Because when you're clear, you're more confident, and when you're more confident, you'll negotiate better.

Getting clear about what you want — and what you don't — is something you can work on any time. In fact, you'll benefit from having your ducks in a row before you even start looking for a job. Don't worry; if you're already interviewing, or even if you have an offer, it's not too late to do this work.

GETTING CLEAR: IT'S *NOT* ALL ABOUT REWARDS

The most important part of your pay negotiation (and arguably, the most overlooked) isn't about pay at all. It's getting clear on what you want out of a job – and an employer.

Are you targeting a specific location, or are you flexible (and how flexible are you)? Do you have principles that you want to see reflected in the place you work (things like sustainability, community service, "work hard/play hard," or social justice)? Are you looking for a large/small, private/public, profit/nonprofit organization? And what types of roles fit your education, experience, and career goals?

It sounds a little counterintuitive, right? Why would you want to narrow things down?

Eliminating the jobs and employers that *aren't* the right fit allows you to focus on the ones that are. It's pretty much impossible to make a case as to why you're the perfect candidate for a wide range of jobs and employers. And when the organization sees you as the perfect candidate, it's easier to negotiate.

When you can clearly articulate what exactly you're looking for, it'll be easier to know when you've got it in your sights.

CLARIFY THE PART THAT *IS* ABOUT REWARDS

For some people, the most important piece of the pay package will be base pay. And until you get to an executive position, base pay will be the biggest part of your pay package, so that's awesome. Base pay often drives other rewards, like bonus target (most are expressed as percentage of base), program eligibility (like deferred compensation programs), and some benefits (like life insurance coverage).

Some folks focus on paid time off, or having the opportunity to make great commissions when they have a fantastic year in sales, or being able to work from home a couple of days a week.

For some people, it's all about the opportunity to grow and develop within the same company, or the mission of the organization, or its culture. That's fine, too, but those are not things you can negotiate. They *are*, however, something you can base your decision on about a company or opportunity.

Take time to figure this out. Before you get an offer!

MINIMUM ACCEPTABLE LEVEL (FLOOR)

Once you're clear on what's important to you, figure out what's minimally acceptable. To you. This means you'll reject the offer if you can't negotiate it above this amount. It doesn't mean your ideal – this is your floor. The least you will accept.

If you've done a good job with your toolset, and you have solid research on what jobs get paid, your base pay floor should be somewhere in the range of salaries you've looked at. And it doesn't need to be the lowest value you find in the data, either.

You should think about a "floor" value for any of the super-important items you've identified. One of the most uncomfortable (and important) things to be able to do in any negotiation is to say "no." Knowing ahead of time what's minimally acceptable — and what you'll say "no" to — can help you stick with your plan and make a better decision.

When you're clear, you're more confident, and when you're more confident, **you'll negotiate better.**

Both of these steps, knowing what's important to you and what's minimally acceptable, are things you can do before you get your offer. In fact, they'll help you screen out opportunities that aren't right for you.

But what if you're finding that your floor is above what you see in the market? If you're not able to find opportunities that have pay and/or benefits above what's minimally acceptable for you, it might be time to reevaluate.

Unless you have truly unique skills and experiences that multiple organizations are clamoring for, it's unlikely you'll be able to set your own market for rewards. Double down on your market research, and focus on what's realistically being offered for the type of work you do. While it sounds impersonal, you're essentially making an exchange: the talents you bring to a job for a total rewards package. Make sure you're being realistic when you set your floor.

CLARITY QUESTIONS/EXERCISES

If you're struggling to figure out what's important to you and what outcomes you need from your salary negotiation, try asking yourself the Clarity Questions below, and complete the Clarity Exercise. Plan some time for this — it isn't quick, check-the-box sort of work.

Clarity Questions.

- What is it about my job that's been most important to me?
- What about my pay and benefits is most important to me?
- What has made me the most frustrated about my previous jobs?
- What has driven me nuts about my previous pay or benefits?
- What about my current/previous job would I miss most?
- What compensation/benefits/other items would make my life easier or better?
- What job- or pay-related stuff do other people think is important that I don't really care about?
- What do other people not care much about that I think is really important?
- How will I know that I've done a great job of negotiating?

Clarity Exercise. Make a list of everything you can think of that relates to the job. Compensation, benefits, intrinsic and extrinsic qualities of the organization, and anything else you think could be important. Highlight the top 10 (or 8, or 15, or whatever makes sense to you). Then rank your list from most important to least important.

You'll want to refer to this list when you assess your offer. Some of your items will be "do they have it or not?" things (like an onsite gym), and others will be "how much are they offering?" things (like paid time off or base pay). If something makes your list of most important things, you'll want to be sure you're thinking about it when you assess your offer and plan your negotiation.

PRO TIPS

- The most important part of pay negotiations isn't about pay at all — it's about getting clear about what you want in a job and from a company.
- Create a prioritized list of items that are important to you to use in your negotiations.
- Think about what's minimally acceptable to you before you get an offer, and be prepared to walk away if you're not able to negotiate an offer that's above your floor.
- Answer the Clarity Questions and complete the Clarity Exercise before you start negotiating.

Chapter 16
Mindset Shifts

Negotiating your pay is HARD. In order to do your best with salary negotiation, it's important to get your head in the right place so you can get the best results possible.

REJECT ASSUMPTIONS

This is the time to jettison all of the assumptions you have about how the conversation is going to go.

"I suck at negotiating!" Let it go.

"They're out to get me and don't want to pay me what I'm worth!" Let it go.

Before any negotiation conversation, you need to look closely at the assumptions you're making about both yourself and the person you're negotiating with and leave behind anything that doesn't serve you.

First, set aside any assumptions about yourself. Stuff like, "I'm bad at negotiating," or "I should just be happy to have an offer," or "I don't deserve a good salary because <whatever dumb thing you want to say here>" are limiting beliefs that don't serve you when you're negotiating.

It's almost certain that the little (big?) irritating voice in your head will come out during the negotiation process. One of the main reasons that happens is your saboteur voice tends to get louder and more insistent when you get closer to something you really want. It's a protective reaction designed to keep the status quo status quo-ing. And to keep you safe from risk. But you need to move past it to get something new.

You also need to release assumptions you have about the person (or organization) you're negotiating with.

Assumptions like, "The employer needs to save money," or "If I ask for more, they'll think I'm pushy," or "If they give me more money, they won't have enough to give a good offer to my friend, who's also applying," are assumptions about the other party that also don't serve you.

But...how do you do it? The main thing here is to realize what's holding you back. It's helpful to write this stuff down. What assumptions do you have about yourself? What are you assuming about the person you're negotiating with? Make lists, and then highlight the ones that don't serve you or your negotiation conversation. And when you've done that, acknowledge them, and make a clear decision to let them go. If you rip up your list of negative assumptions and put them in the trash, that physical act will help your brain put them aside.

Kick assumptions to the curb before you start negotiating!

RESET YOUR MINDSET

There are a host of mindsets that don't serve us, especially in pay negotiations. Shift these unhelpful mindsets to ones that can really help you.

From Competition to Collaboration. What would happen if you thought of your recruiter or hiring manager as a collaborator in negotiations instead of an adversary? When you're both working together toward the same goal — a great match with a package you both feel great about — negotiations don't feel as scary or negative. A caveat here: don't give up your power in the interest of being nice. You can be clear and firm about what you need and still be collaborative.

From Scarcity to Abundance. People who focus on scarcity tend to worry about having "enough" (money, time, food, shoes, Pokémon, etc.). When you're in scarcity mode, you're more likely to protect or hoard what resources you have. This shows up in salary negotiation when people don't want to negotiate because they're afraid of losing the offer. Or when they keep negotiating an offer for a job they don't want so they can have multiple offers.

In contrast, the abundance mindset feels expansive and free. When you enter negotiations knowing there are many paths to success, it's easier to keep an open mind and see multiple solutions. When your decision doesn't hinge on a single number (like base pay), and you're ready to look at a combined package to fulfill your needs, there are many more ways of getting to a great resolution to your negotiations.

From Waiting to Progress. There are so many ways to wait and not take action in the job search and negotiation spaces. There's a reason people say "Progress beats perfection." If you're waiting for that one perfect offer, you may pass up opportunities that you could negotiate into something wonderful. Better to move forward than procrastinate!

The interview and pay negotiation process is your first, best opportunity to make a **great impression** on the company.

From Options to Choosing. This one's a little counter-intuitive. Don't you want ALL THE OPTIONS? In reality, keeping options open takes a lot of energy. Are you keeping options on the table that are taking your energy away from the choices you really care about? If you know that a job or opportunity isn't a good match for you, and that you'd never take it, consider letting it go to make room for the right ones.

From Fear to Possibility. So many fears crop up with salary negotiation. "What if they pull my offer because I ask for more money?" (By the way, it bears repeating that I've never in all my years of experience seen this happen.) Or,

"What if they say no?" or "What will they think of me if I don't negotiate well?"

The great news is that by reading this book, you're already moving away from the fear mindset. If you can reframe your mindset into one of possibility – like, "What is possible for me if this negotiation goes well?" or "What if they say 'yes'?" it's going to help you a ton.

From Security to Opportunity. A security mindset can keep you from taking risks. And if you eliminate all risk, you'll have certainty, that's true, but you'll stay stagnant (at best). Noticing and taking advantage of the opportunities that arise in pay negotiations requires a different mindset.

If you're willing to take risks, there's a possibility of failure, but there's also a possibility of something new and awesome. Calculated risk-taking in salary negotiations can minimize your downside and maximize your opportunities!

KNOW HOW YOU WANT TO SHOW UP

When you think about the person who you'll be negotiating with, what do you want them to notice about you? Answering that question will help you know how you want to show up.

You might want them to notice that you're competent and articulate. Or that you're someone they'd enjoy collaborating with. Or that you're knowledgeable and organized.

And once you figure out how you want to show up, be intentional about it. Focus on it. What can you do in your preparation so that you can showcase those qualities? You don't need to run around shouting, "I'm so easy to work with!" — if you are kind (even if you're firm), return calls promptly, and treat everyone in the process with respect, guess what? You're showing it. Showing beats telling, hands down.

The interview and pay negotiation process is your first, best opportunity to make a great impression on the company. If you're looking at a leadership position, it's doubly important to be conscious of how you're showing up.

What do you want to be known for as a leader? Act that way. From the start. With everybody. I can tell you from experience that HR folks provide lots of feedback to hiring managers on how they're treated by candidates. When that's good feedback, it can really help you onboard in your new role. If it's bad...not so much.

Some folks I talk with about pay negotiation think it's all about rolling over or not asking for what they want, all in service of being "nice." Remember, it's not personal, for you or for them. Sure, it might be easier for them (at least in the short-term) if you agree to everything in your offer. But if you're not happy with it and say "yes" anyway, that doesn't serve you *or* the organization in the longer-term.

You shouldn't give up your negotiating power in order to be perceived as easy to work with.

PRO TIPS

- Examine the assumptions you're making about yourself and the person you're negotiating with, and dump them.
- Mindsets of collaboration, possibility, and opportunity can serve you well in negotiations.
- Set an intention for how you want to show up in your negotiation, and make any preparations you need to set yourself up for success with that intention.
- Don't give up your negotiating power in order to be perceived as "nice."

Chapter 17

It's NOT Personal

Negotiating your pay can be pretty emotional for just about everybody. But one thing my years working in compensation for some of the best companies out there proved to me is that pay is not personal. And neither is pay negotiation.

A big salary doesn't mean you're worth more as a person than someone who makes less than you do. And vice versa.

Bottom line (and one of the most important takeaways from this book): your offer and your pay say more about how your company values the role you're being paid to do than how much you are worth as a person.

It's really not personal!

A job offer is all about how the company values the JOB; it's not about how valuable YOU are as a person.

Seriously. It's not about you.

Even though the outcome affects you personally, the negotiation is not personal. The more you can wrap your head around this concept, the better it will serve you in salary negotiations.

YOUR NEGOTIATION ISN'T PERSONAL

As long as you're adhering to Salary Negotiation Rule #1 (Don't Be a Jerk), your negotiation isn't going to be about who you are as a person.

Of course, there are skills you can learn (you're learning them right now!) to help you negotiate better, and from a place of confidence, which is awesome. But those are tools.

Your recruiter isn't sitting at their desk, rubbing their hands together like some evil mastermind, thinking, "How can I make this candidate miserable? Bwahaha!" They want, more than anything else, to create a great match between you (the candidate) and the organization. And they want you coming into your new job excited and energized.

When a recruiter or hiring manager tells you they're not able to go higher on the salary/bonus/vacation/relocation, it's because that's what's true for them. They're not playing mind games. They're not trying to trick you. If their best offer isn't what you want or need, you can walk away.

YOUR OFFER ISN'T PERSONAL

Lots of folks I talk with about pay negotiation want to use their offers as proof of their own personal value. This happens with recent graduates, C-suite executives, and with people at every level in between.

Stop that. It isn't true.

Companies are pretty impersonal with this stuff. Trust me on this. They want to get great talent into their organizations, and they don't want to overpay. And contrary to what many people think, most companies don't want to underpay, either, because they'll wind up losing their great talent, which will ultimately cost them more. They want to pay at market. The going rate. Not more; not less.

Of course, there are a handful of employers who take the low-cost/pay-below-market approach, but for most of them, it can only be temporary. They're limiting their talent pool to people who will accept below-market pay, and they have to live with higher turnover than their market-paying competition. It's a short-sighted and short-term approach.

When your offer isn't as high as you think it should be, it's almost always going to be because you and the organization have different ideas about what the *work you do* is worth. It might be a mismatch with the level of the job, or it might be because the company doesn't understand the skills and experience that it takes to do the job, or it could be that the organization doesn't want to invest in the role or the expertise, or their pay philosophy may emphasize elements that you don't value (like equity over base pay).

That's all okay.

You may — or may not — be able to change their perspective on it. And if you can't, you'll have to decide if it makes sense to take the job knowing that's the case.

A job offer is all about how the company values the JOB; it's **not** about how valuable YOU are as a person.

I had a client who interviewed for a job in her hometown and gave her pay expectations with that in mind. When the company offered her a similar role in a much higher cost of living city, they offered her the amount she had originally asked for. She was very upset that they didn't increase the offer before presenting it. But it wasn't personal.

The original offer was within their pay range in the higher cost location, so they didn't see the need to increase it automatically. She shifted the energy she was devoting to being upset into energy that fueled her negotiations. Once she changed her mindset to not take it personally, she was able to ask for — and get — a much more robust package.

PRO TIPS

- Pay negotiations aren't personal, and they're not some weird mind trick or conspiracy, either.
- Your offer reflects how the organization values the job, not how it values you as a person.
- When you're able to shift your perspective and take things less personally, you'll be able to take more emotion out of your talks and negotiate better.

Chapter 18

Mindset Client Success Story

To highlight the importance of Mindset, I'm sharing another client success story.

My client was negotiating an offer with a wonderful company, one they'd always dreamed of working with. When they received the offer, I helped them assess it and compare it to what they were already making.

The offer from the new company was awesome. So, my client said to me, "I'm just going to take it. It's a good offer, and I don't want them to think I'm difficult to work with." (Remember – if you negotiate respectfully, they will NOT think you're difficult!)

We talked about the benefits of negotiating and which items they wanted to tackle, and we created a game plan to get after them. They decided to negotiate base pay and sign-on bonus.

The client wasn't confident they would be able to get the company to increase the base pay — they'd had discussions throughout the interview process about it, and the base offer had already moved significantly higher than what was first discussed over the interview period. But their strategy for asking was based on the higher cost of labor in the new location, and also to make a higher sign-on bonus an attractive alternative for the company if they couldn't move on base pay.

To negotiate their sign-on bonus, we looked at the value of what they were walking away from in the old company. It was slightly more than the offered sign-on bonus. We then discussed how their fears ("I'm not good at negotiating!" and "They'll think I'm difficult to work with if I negotiate") were holding them back from asking for what they wanted.

They used the 7 Magic Words ("What kind of flexibility do you have?") and asked for more, based on what they were walking away from at their current company.

The future employer wasn't able to move the base pay higher, but they offered a significant bump in the sign-on bonus.

Guess what? The new bonus was a whopping 56% increase (multiple 5-figures) from the original offer!

My client was delighted at how their negotiation paid off. Big time.

Chapter 19

Mindset Q&A

Q: What's the most important thing to negotiate?

A: It depends on what's most important to you. Really!

Q: When an HR person gives you a pay range, is that real?

A: In my experience, HR folks don't lie on stuff like this. It doesn't serve them to give you bad info — it reflects poorly on them and the company. But things do sometimes change.

Occasionally, the way the organization thinks of the job (and its level) can shift over time, or their expectations about what they're able to offer can change. If you do hear different numbers from different people, get curious, and ask. Don't automatically jump to the conclusion that there's an active conspiracy. Do pay attention, though, to other signs that there may not be alignment internally about the job.

Q: I simply *have to* get this negotiation right! Everything depends on it!

A: Whoa! Let's slow down a bit here. When you put a ton of pressure on yourself about negotiations, you're likely to bring more emotion into the conversation, which will make it harder to show up the way you want to (and to do a great job negotiating).

Get a little emotional distance by pretending you're negotiating on behalf of a friend. That will take some of the emotion out of the equation.

Q: If I ask for higher base pay, but I don't get it, and I still wind up accepting the job, I'll feel stupid. That makes me not want to do it. Why should I?

A: Asking for stuff you don't get is part of negotiation. You may not get what you've asked for, especially in the later stages of negotiation when the organization has already made some concessions. If there's still something you're aiming for, go ahead and ask (but as always, be polite)!

If you don't get it, it's not like your offer goes down to zero. But what if you get it? That would be even more awesome!

Q: I'm very anxious! My recruiter told me I'd have an offer emailed to me on Monday, and it's Wednesday already. I gave notice to my current company yesterday. What should I do?

A: It's time to reach out to the recruiter again. It's certainly possible — probable, even — that something got in the way of them meeting their commitment to get the offer letter to you. If you're not able to track them down, it's fine to reach out to the hiring manager, too. (And next time, don't give notice until you have your offer completely negotiated with an offer letter and start date in hand!)

Q: I'm really worried about my negotiation conversation. I'm really bad with this stuff, and I know the company will try to take advantage of me. Why should I even try to get what I want in the negotiations?

A: Get rid of those assumptions! You may be inexperienced, but great preparation, including practicing what you want to say, will help tons. And the company wants you to come to work for them and to be excited about it. It's not a nefarious plot.

You should negotiate your pay to get more of what you want...and to get more experience so it's easier to negotiate in the future.

Q: Since I'm in sales, it's important that the company knows I can negotiate well. How can I show them what I've got?

A: That depends on what you want to show them. If it's that you can be firm, professional, collaborative, and kind in the negotiation process, go for it! If you're thinking more along the lines of head-to-head, "I-win-you-lose" stuff, that's not nearly as effective in salary talks, so save it.

Q: My target company has given me a good offer. I'm not going to try to get more – I don't want to start a new job with them thinking I'm not grateful.

A: It's always great to show your gratitude by letting the company know that you're thrilled to have an offer before you start asking for more. Companies do expect candidates to negotiate; don't throw away a great opportunity to practice your negotiating skills.

Even if you don't get additional pay, getting more comfortable with the negotiation process can serve you down the line.

Q: How do you get an honest answer about how many hours a week people work in your prospective company?

A: Chances are pretty good that you'll be interviewing with at least one potential peer (and if you're not, ask if you can). Talk with them about the team and organization culture, and ask them directly about the expectations for hours, both in "normal" times as well as in high-demand times.

Q: I've been interviewing for a job, and while I'm really excited about it, I think it's a bigger job than I first thought when I gave the company my pay expectations. Am I screwed?

A: Not at all. It's absolutely fine to bring this up with the recruiter or hiring manager. You can always use the phrase: "Based on what I now know of the job, I'm targeting $XX. How close can we get to that?"

Q: I love the job, the company, and the manager, but the base is 20% below my minimum acceptable rate. What should I do?

A: That's a big difference! But with everything this job has going for it, it's worth trying to negotiate. Use the "what to say" phrases to try to get them to move the pay up. Who knows? You might be able to get your pay to a place where you need it to be.

But if you can't come to a solution that works for you both, be prepared to walk away. And if you do walk away, let them know how much you'd love to work with them if an opportunity comes up that would be a better fit.

PART 4

PUTTING IT ALL TOGETHER

Okay! Now that we have all of the elements you need to negotiate your offer (Toolset, Skillset, and Mindset), let's put everything together and put it into action.

What's in this section…

Chapter 20: Creating Your Game Plan

The best format for pay negotiations. Deciding which questions to ask. Planning how to discuss the changes you'd like to see. Planning for follow-up. The importance of ending well.

Chapter 21: Negotiation Prep

Getting your data ready. Designing your approach. Preparing your talking points. Putting your tools in order. Clearing your mind.

Chapter 22: Special Circumstances

Advice for those in special job types including: recent college graduates, sales people, executives, contract players, volunteers, freelancers, and consultants. How pay works differently for those working in startups and nonprofits.

Chapter 23: You're Done. Now What?

How you know you're done. How (and why) to gracefully bow out of the negotiation process. Why celebration matters. Learning from your experience.

Chapter 24: Putting It All Together Client Success Story

How a client put toolset, skillset, and mindset together to increase their offer by more than $120,000.

Chapter 25: Putting It All Together Q&A

Questions I get about stuff in the Putting It All Together section (and how I answer them).

Chapter 20

Creating Your Game Plan

Let's talk about how to get your negotiation done. The basic plan is to clarify what you don't understand, discuss the areas you'd like to see changed, and make a plan for following up.

PHONE, IN-PERSON, OR EMAIL?

I always recommend that my clients do salary negotiation over the phone. Phone negotiations work well because you can have any supporting information you want in front of you, you can move the negotiation more quickly, and you can listen to hear how what you're saying is landing with the person you're negotiating with.

It's hard to convey tone or emotion over email, and you don't get feedback in the moment. In-person negotiations are difficult for most people, since it's harder to mask emotional responses (on both sides). If you need to use one of these methods, pay careful attention to how you're showing up.

ASK QUESTIONS

You are definitely going to have questions. That's only natural. If you don't understand something that's included in your offer, ask the hiring manager or HR person to explain things to you.

The questions list you put together in **Chapter 7 | Understanding Your Offer** will have all the things you need to know more about. And you should have questions here! It's normal (and expected). Stuff like "When does the bonus pay out every year?" and "When would I be eligible for my next pay review?" are great questions.

You should NOT ask questions that are easily answered in the information the organization sent you. If you need clarification, that's totally fine, but don't ask if there's dental insurance coverage if they sent you a benefits brochure with that information clearly stated in it.

Once you're at the offer stage, the company is really hoping you say yes, and getting answers to your questions can help you feel more comfortable.

I recommend you divide your questions into two lists. The first is a list of things that you must know before you can adequately assess your offer. The second list will be the things that are nice to know, but the answers won't necessarily impact your decision. Where these questions fall will depend on what's important to you, but here are some examples.

For your sanity's sake, you must make sure to nail down **how and when the next step will happen**.

Questions to Understand. Answers to these questions help you understand your offer better and decide whether to accept or negotiate each element. Typically included here are questions about the size of your bonus opportunity and the typical payout for the past few years, whether or not the role is paid for overtime, and eligibility for long-term incentives or equity.

Nice-to-Know. While this stuff isn't necessarily crucial to the negotiation process, the answers to these questions will help you to move forward with a clear understanding of your package. Things like timing of annual bonus payout, start date, when you can expect your first paycheck or sign-on bonus check, or when equity is awarded could fall into this category.

Don't forget the homework piece. If you have tons of questions that can be easily answered by reading what the organization already gave you, that can get irritating after a while. You want to save that energy for discussing the changes you'd like to see in your package!

DISCUSS CHANGES YOU'D LIKE

You've done a great job of understanding and assessing your offer; now it's time to address the things you'd like to see changed in the offer.

The key to this piece is being clear and firm about what you want without being a jerk.

- "The offer letter says the base pay is $85,000. Based on what I know of the role and the market, I'm targeting $115,000. How close can we get to that?" = CLEAR, FIRM, NOT A JERK
- "The offer letter says the base pay is $85,000. That's both ridiculous and insulting. What else can you do for me?" = NOT CLEAR, NOT FIRM, DEFINITELY A JERK

As you negotiate, use your prioritized "big-to-small" list you created, and move through your items. Again, focus on the energy of collaboration, and be aware of the impression you're creating.

For executives, I'd recommend negotiating the compensation and benefits elements in one conversation, and talk about employment agreement items in a separate conversation, if possible. For most of my clients, that's the natural way the conversations flow, and it allows you to have two, substantive conversations, rather than trying to cram everything into one.

While you may get answers to some of your requests while you're on the phone, don't count on it. It's pretty unusual for the recruiter or hiring manager to be able to meet all of your needs on the spot. It's far more likely that they'll need to go back to the hiring manager (or just to take some time to look at internal impacts) before coming back with an answer.

There's more info about what to say (and what not to) in **Chapter 11 | What to Say,** and you'll find lots of helpful phrases in the Q&A at the end of each section.

LEVERAGING ONE OFFER TO GET ANOTHER

Clients often ask me if it's okay to use an offer they have in hand to get another employer to hurry up their process. You can definitely try, but it may or may not work. Companies have their own timelines, and if they're not ready to extend an offer, they're not.

It's absolutely fine to let a prospective employer know that you've received another offer and that if they'd like you to consider working for them, you'll need to have their offer in hand before you respond to the offer from the other company.

You'll likely have better luck in leveraging a higher offer from a company that's *not* your favorite to get better pay with the one you want most. But it may not be worth the hassle.

Be honest with yourself. If the offer you have now is the one you really want, it's totally fine to focus on negotiating that one, and if you can get to an offer you like, go for it. There's no requirement to play one company's offer against another's.

Whatever you decide, be sure to let the other company know once you've accepted your dream offer.

FOLLOW-UP PLAN

This is one of the areas many people forget, and can cause the biggest stress headaches. For your sanity's sake, you *must* make sure to nail down how and when the next step will happen.

Sometimes, the person you're negotiating with will let you know when you can expect to hear from them, but often, it goes unsaid. If you're nearing the end of your conversation and the subject hasn't come up, ask what the next steps are. And if they don't specify a date when you can expect to hear back, offer to connect with them on a specific date (try proposing something two or three business days out).

END WELL

Let's talk a bit about endings. In Daniel Pink's book, *When*, his research showed that how things end is more important than beginnings or middles. And that applies to salary negotiation, too.

Always strive to have a positive ending to the conversation. One of the best ways to do that is to talk about how excited you are about the opportunity, to express that you're confident you'll be able to come to an agreement, and to thank the person you're talking with for their hard work in this process.

Don't forget to end the conversation on an up note!

PRO TIPS

- If you have the option, negotiate over the phone.
- Ask questions so you understand your package.
- Discuss the changes you'd like to see clearly and firmly, and be nice.
- Talk about next steps, and agree on a date to follow up.
- End well — make sure your recruiter or hiring manager knows you're excited about the opportunity.

Chapter 21

Negotiation Prep

Now that you have your game plan, how should you prepare for the negotiation conversations themselves? There's a ton of things to do. Time you spend in negotiation prep is well-spent.

You'll be both more confident and more competent at negotiation time when you have your data, approach, talking points, tools, and mindset ready.

PREP YOUR DATA

You've worked hard to figure out what the market rate for the job is, your bottom-line numbers, and what you're hoping to negotiate. Before you get on a call, get everything onto a single piece of paper. You don't want to be riffling through your notes and getting distracted in the conversation. Make sure your information is clear, easy to read, and at your fingertips.

PREP YOUR APPROACH

Think about how you'll collaborate with the person you're negotiating with. If you have been working with them throughout the hiring process, it'll be easier to envision how to collaborate with them. If the person is new to you, it's important to think through how you'll build rapport.

And remember my suggestion to negotiate like you would on behalf of a friend so you can take some emotion out of the process.

One thing I recommend to clients is to think about your approach in four phases:

1. Excitement
2. Questions
3. Requests
4. Confidence

Always start the negotiation by telling the other party that you're thrilled/happy/delighted to have an offer. Don't make them wonder. It sets the stage well.

Next, ask the questions you've prepared from your game plan so you can understand your offer better.

Then, go through the changes you'd like to see, also from your game plan.

Last, express confidence that you (both of you) will be able to come to a solution that works for you and the company. End on an up note, and don't forget to figure out the follow-up plan!

Boom.

PREP YOUR TALKING POINTS

Of course, you don't know exactly what the person you're negotiating with will say. But you can — and should — anticipate the key talking points of the conversation.

To the extent possible, you'll want to steer and shape the conversation. That's why you got clear about what you wanted and figured out the order you want to negotiate things. Of course, shaping and steering doesn't mean bullying and talking over folks, but when you have an agenda and prepared talking points, chances are good you'll be able to get to the things you want to talk about.

What questions do you expect they'll ask? What points would you like to get across? Which questions do you need answers to? Are there things you agreed to talk about in this meeting?

The best way to prep your talking points is to write them out and practice them. Out loud. And if you have a close pal you can practice with, so much the better. The goal is to be able to say what you want without stumbling over the words (or reading them from a page like a robot).

PREP YOUR TOOLS

We've all heard (or lived) the horror stories: you're in the middle of a negotiation and your phone dies. Or your pen runs out of ink just as you're writing something important down. Or you forget what you wanted to say.

While you can't control everything, you can plan for lots of potential mishaps. If you're meeting by phone, make sure it's fully charged and you'll be in a place with great reception. Plan to take your call in a quiet place, and minimize potential interruptions.

If you're meeting via video, check to be sure your audio and video are functioning, and that your lighting makes it easy to see your face. And if you share internet service with a gamer, ask them to stop playing while you're on your video call. (I know, I know, but it can make a huge difference in your audio and video quality!)

Bring at least two pens or pencils and a notepad with plenty of pages. And last, but by no means least, have your list of questions, talking points, and backup documentation easily accessible (and large enough to read easily).

And if things don't go the way you expect, be flexible and have a sense of humor. Remember, every interaction with your potential (or current) employer is an opportunity to show them how great it would be to work with you.

PREP YOUR EXIT

You always want to plan for things to go well during negotiations, but there are times when they won't. If there's no way for the company you're negotiating with to meet your minimally acceptable terms, or if you get a bad feeling about the job or the organization, or if something just isn't right, you need to plan for what you'll say and do.

Practicing what you'll say as you decline an offer is more important than you may think — it can be a very emotionally charged moment, which makes it a ton harder to come up with the right words on the spot.

If you think you may be in a position to say "no" to an offer, write up a sentence or two and practice them before you get on the call. A couple of ways to approach this tough conversation are:

- "I really appreciate all the work you and the company have put into the offer, but at this point, I think we're too far apart to come to an agreement that will suit us both. I hope you'll keep me in mind for other opportunities that might be a better fit for what I'm looking for."
- "Thank you so much for all your help on this! After a lot of consideration, I've decided that this role isn't a good fit for me, and it's time for me to bow out of the offer process. I wish you all the best in finding your perfect candidate."

The best way to prep your talking points is to write them out and practice them. **Out loud.**

PREP YOUR BODY

It's easy to forget these things, but befor you get on your call, be sure to...

- Go to the bathroom
- Grab a glass or bottle of water (when you're nervous, your throat can go dry in an instant
- Have a cough drop or throat lozenge handy.

PREP YOUR BRAIN

And by that, I mean "meditate."

Really? Meditation? For negotiation prep?

Absolutely.

Yeah, it sounds a little "woo," but be sure to take time before your negotiations — even just five minutes will help — to meditate or to sit quietly, if meditation isn't your jam. Meditation can help you get out of freakout mode and into a space of calm, relaxed confidence.

After your meditation/quiet sitting/deep breathing time is up, think about how you want to show up. Whether it's confident, curious, knowledgeable, able to stand up for yourself, a combo, or something else that makes sense for you, imagine yourself in the negotiations making exactly the impression you intend to.

My clients tell me that even a five-minute session meditating or sitting quietly before they get on the phone with their potential employer helps them focus better, be present for the conversation, and make the kind of impact they want.

Honestly, this is a great practice to use when you're approaching any type of high-stakes and/or emotional discussion, presentation, or meeting.

Once you've meditated and focused on your impact, you can get on that call and do your best!

PRO TIPS

- Take time to plan the questions you want to ask and the points you want to get across. And practice them. Out loud. A lot.
- Prepare your tools (phone, video, pens, question list, supporting documents, etc.) to eliminate as many potential mishaps as possible.
- Be ready to say "no" if you need to.
- Take at least five minutes to meditate or sit quietly before you get on a negotiation call, and focus on how you want to show up.

Chapter 22
Special Circumstances

I get it. You're special! Most of the advice in this book applies to most jobs and situations most of the time. But sometimes…not. Here are some cases where pay and benefits are treated a little differently, and your negotiations may be different, too.

RECENT COLLEGE GRADS

If you got this book to help you negotiate your first job out of college, good for you! Maximizing your pay in early jobs can pay off in higher salaries over the course of your career. Nice work!

That said, it may be a bit harder to negotiate your starting salary earlier in your career than later on. That's because many companies have set rates they offer new grads by position. With the rise of the Fair Pay Act, employers have to be able to justify the reasons that people in the same job are paid differently. To give yourself your best shot at negotiating, make sure your potential employer knows the things in your background that could justify you getting paid more, like certifications or specialized experience.

Even if you're not able to negotiate a higher salary as a recent college graduate, you may be able to get a bigger sign-on bonus or relocation allowance. Use this opportunity to practice negotiation — you'll feel more comfortable doing it later!

SALES ROLES

Many sales roles have some sort of sales incentives or commissions element in their pay packages. Your company will likely offer incentives/commissions instead of the bonus programs non-sales folks get. Because of the size and opportunity of some of these incentives, it's really important to understand how they work.

When you're first starting a new sales role, your company may guarantee your bonus for a period of time or offer you a draw against your commission.

Make sure you know what you're getting into and when things transition. Other terms to clarify include when bonuses are paid out, timing of commission payouts, what the cap on your earnings is (if any), and how customer returns or cancellations are handled.

EXECUTIVES

As you climb the ladder of a publicly traded company, long-term incentives (LTI) play a bigger and bigger role. It's super-important that you clearly understand the long-term elements in your pay package, whether they're stock options, restricted stock, or cash (or some sort of combination).

Your LTI should inform how — and more importantly, when — you plan your career moves. What are you giving up/gaining when you move from one company to another? How does LTI impact your plans for retirement?

Some types of jobs have **special considerations**, and you should get clear on them before negotiating — or accepting — an offer.

If you're at a senior level in your company, you're more likely to be asked to sign an employment agreement, which will dictate the terms of your employment. You may also be required to sign a non-compete agreement, where you'd commit to not working for a competitor for a certain length of time in return for some sort of compensation.

While I'm not going to go into the details of these types of agreements here, it's important that you know what they are, what the terms mean, and how they might affect you. It's easy to just skip over the details and sign, but you really must understand their terms before signing.

If you're one of the "top five" executives in a publicly-traded company (CEO, CFO, or three other most highly-compensated roles), your pay will be disclosed in the company's annual report (specifically, the Compensation Discussion and Analysis, or CD&A, section, which you'll find in the proxy). You'll also be able to check out how top five execs at other companies are paid by looking in their annual reports. You'll find lots of great info about how executive short-term and long-term incentives work at the company in the annual report, too.

STARTUPS

Lots of startups pump up the equity to make up for lower base pay (or anything that's not market-competitive in their offer). That makes it doubly important to be sure you understand how equity will be handled in different scenarios. It's not likely that any one startup will go IPO — it's far more likely that the company will be purchased or acquired (or go under).

Make sure that whatever your pay package looks like *without* equity makes sense for you, too. While it would be awesome if your company hit it big, it might not.

NONPROFITS

Pay at nonprofits is almost always lower than pay for similar roles in for-profit companies. Short-term bonuses aren't as common at nonprofits, and long-term incentives are pretty rare, except at the largest organizations. I don't love this, but it's the reality.

That said, it's still okay to negotiate your pay and to ask for market-competitive base pay. With salary data getting so much easier to access, I have seen base pay for nonprofits come up over the years, which is a very good thing!

CONTRACT PLAYERS

Negotiating contracts for athletes, movie stars, and other similar jobs is a whole different animal, and many of the things we're talking about in the book may not apply to you. You'll want to engage with an agent or attorney to help you understand how things work, what your obligations are, and where you can — and should — negotiate.

VOLUNTEER/UNPAID POSITIONS

Okay, so most of the stuff we talk about regarding pay won't apply to you. But setting boundaries and negotiating your duties and work conditions certainly does. As a volunteer, you may have better success at negotiating some of the things you want — and that negotiating practice will serve you over the long haul!

FREELANCERS & CONSULTANTS

If you're a freelancer or consultant, most of the Toolset section won't apply to you. But lots of the Skillset section will, and pretty much all of the Mindset section will, too.

My next book is about setting (and raising) freelance and consulting rates, and if you'd like to be on the mailing list to get updates, please sign up here: **www.katedixon.org/PayUpBook**.

PRO TIPS

- Most tips included in this book will work for a wide variety of roles.
- Some types of jobs have special considerations, and you should get clear on them before negotiating — or accepting — an offer.

Chapter 23

You're Done. Now What?

Holy cow. You did it! Nothing's hanging over your head — you're complete. Congratulations!

HOW YOU'LL KNOW YOU'RE DONE

Sometimes it's hard to know when you're really done with negotiations. Is it when you get your offer letter? No.

Is it after you've had that first, agonizing negotiation conversation? Not yet.

Is it when you have a conversation where your new employer gives you everything you want (or at least a revised offer you can feel great about accepting? Almost...but not quite.

You are done with your salary negotiations when you get *written confirmation* of your updated offer. While many organizations will do this with an updated offer letter, some prefer to put the negotiated details into an email. Which is fine, by the way. You simply must get anything you've agreed to in writing before you formally accept the job.

If your future employer doesn't feel the need to put things in writing, you put it in writing. Email your recruiter or hiring manager (or better yet, both) with the details, and ask them to reply with an approval confirmation. My attorney friends assure me that the email approval works the same way as an offer letter if you ever need proof of the agreements you made, but you should check with your legal counsel on the particulars of your situation, too.

If you just can't get to an offer that suits both you and your prospective employer, you need to take another route. Which leads us to...

CUTTING YOUR LOSSES, GRACEFULLY

Sometimes, things don't work out the way you planned. And that's okay.

What's not okay is working and working to get an offer from a company or for a job that you're not really interested in. At a certain point, you need to cut your losses. And by that, I mean stop spending more of your precious time nurturing a relationship with an organization that you're not into. Or for a job that's not right.

If you thought both the job and the company were the right fit, but you couldn't come to terms on the offer, ask the recruiter or hiring manager to keep you in mind if their budget changes or if they open up a job that you'd be a better fit for at a more senior level. Make sure they know that you'd love to work with them in the future.

You are done with your salary negotiations when you get **written confirmation** of your updated offer.

If the job isn't a good fit, but you love the company, leave the discussions on good terms, and ask them to contact you if something more in line with your goals comes up. And plan to follow up with them in a few months.

If you can't see yourself ever working for the organization, you should still work on leaving the discussions gracefully. Hiring managers and recruiters do change companies, and the recruiting community is smaller than you might think.

Leaving the employer waiting for a reply from you is never the right approach. When you bow out, make sure they know you're doing it.

CELEBRATION

Finally! Cue the confetti and Champagne! (Or whatever it is that makes it feel like a celebration to you!)

Take some time to celebrate all you've accomplished with negotiating your package. It's easy to just breeze by it in your preparations to leave your current job and start up your new one. But you *need* to celebrate. You've just applied a bunch of hard-earned learning, and you need to give your brain the reinforcement it craves. You'll be reinforcing the neural pathways you created as you behaved in new ways, and that will make those behaviors easier the next time you're in a similar situation.

POST-NEGOTIATION LEARNING

After celebration, the next most important thing to think about is what you learned from your experience. What worked well? What didn't work so well? What would you do differently next time?

Write it all down — chances are good that you won't be negotiating salary again any time soon, and you don't want to try to remember all of it in a couple of years when you need this information again.

PRO TIPS

- Get everything you've agreed to in your pay negotiations in writing. All of it.
- Sometimes, you need to cut your losses. Do it with grace.
- Be sure to celebrate your wins — it reinforces your newly awesome behaviors.
- Lock in your learning by jotting some notes about how you want to approach negotiations in the future.

Chapter 24

Putting It All Together Client Success Story

This last client story shows how everything works together, from Toolset, to Skillset, to Mindset.

My client was a senior executive who had been referred to me by another leader familiar with my work. We knew this would be a complex negotiation that would cover both an offer letter and multiple employment agreements.

Since the client had spent most of their career at a single company, they were concerned that they didn't have enough information about the market or how pay worked in other organizations. They knew they would be giving up certain rewards elements to go to the new company and that the new organization had other pay and benefits items unfamiliar to them.

Like many accomplished business leaders, it was difficult for them to enter into negotiations knowing how little they knew about the process or what might be happening behind the scenes.

When the client first came to me, we talked about what outcomes they wanted to get from their negotiation (a market-competitive holistic package with relocation benefits that would take care of their family).

We also discussed market pay for their position, how the negotiation process typically works, and how we could work together to get them the best results.

After reviewing their package, the biggest gaps they wanted to close were in the annual bonus and base pay.

They decided to approach the negotiation in segments with pay elements first, relocation items second, and finally the employment agreement. This multi-phase approach is especially effective with complex packages — it gives each conversation focus, and it's less overwhelming (for them and for you!).

A side note: For complex employee agreements, I always recommend bringing legal experts in to consult. Their expertise is invaluable in making changes to confidentiality agreements, non-compete clauses, and severance items.

For the first phase of negotiations, my client prepared by getting clear on what they wanted to ask for (more base pay and bonus) and the minimum they were willing to accept (the original offer with no changes). We discussed likely scenarios, they wrote down the responses they wanted to give, then they practiced what they wanted to say. A lot.

And then before their negotiation conversation, they sat in a quiet spot, meditated, and focused on how they wanted to show up for the conversation: calm, firm, and showing their leadership presence.

In the negotiation discussion, the person my client was negotiating with let them know that the company was not likely to be able to move the base and bonus to the level that the client asked for, but that they would go back to see what was possible.

The offer that came back was not exactly what we expected, but it was a welcome surprise. My client successfully negotiated a modest (5%) increase to their base pay and bonus, along with a staggering 50% increase to their equity award. While they had hoped for even more of an increase to base and bonus, the company's sky-high jump in equity made it easy to accept.

With the pay elements part of the negotiation successfully behind them, they moved on to negotiating elements of their relocation package, and then to their employment agreement.

My client's results were impressive. They successfully negotiated multiple elements of pay, relocation, and employment agreement. They used negotiations as an opportunity to demonstrate their collaboration skills and leadership presence. They created allies in their new organization even before the start date.

And their negotiations netted them more than $120,000 in value.

Chapter 25

Putting It All Together Q&A

Q: Could you give me a quick rundown of what I should be doing in my negotiations?

A: First, let them know how excited you are to have an offer. Then, move to your questions to make sure you understand the offer, and discuss any requests you have. Then, express confidence that you'll be able to come to a solution. And last but not least, set a time to talk again (so you don't have to wonder when it might happen).

Q: I've got a great offer from company A — it's at the top of the range I was targeting, with great benefits. But I'm waiting on an offer from company B, which I've spent

loads of time interviewing with. How do I push company B to make an offer so I can compare?

A: It's totally okay to let company B know that you have an offer in hand from company A (although I wouldn't tell them who company A is, even if they ask). You can ask company B if they're in a position to make an offer.

If you'd rather work for B, let them know that, too, but don't try to get them to make an offer just for the sake of having it if A's the company you'd rather work for.

Q: My offer isn't what I hoped it would be, but I really need this job, and my dad said that the company will withdraw my offer if I try to negotiate. Is this true?

A: In all of my career, I've never seen an offer withdrawn for negotiating in good faith. The only times I've seen an offer withdrawn have been when the applicant misrepresented themselves (like, lied on their resume or application).

Q: My negotiation call is in 30 minutes, and I. Am. Freaking. Out. Help!

A: Take a few minutes to meditate or just sit quietly. You can try box breathing, where you inhale for four seconds, hold your breath for four seconds, exhale for four seconds, and hold for four seconds (but do this for a few minutes at a go). This will help calm you down and focus. Think about how you want to show up, and remember that you've prepared for this conversation!

You've got this!

Q: I'm interviewing for a job in a nonprofit I love. I've never worked for a nonprofit, though — what should I expect from a compensation and benefits perspective?

A: You probably know this already, but both pay and benefits tend to be lower at nonprofits than at for-profit companies. On the other hand, it's rare to get the same sense of mission-focus from a for-profit company. The size and scope of the nonprofit will play a huge part in determining what the pay and benefits will be, but you'll need to ask — and look at your offer materials closely.

Q: Since we have the Equal Pay Act, I'm pretty sure all I'll need to negotiate is my paid time off and benefits. Right?

A: Well...not exactly. There are couple of things for you to consider First, are you going into a job that there are already tons of folks in? Like a management training program or a staff accountant (when there are already a bunch of them)?

If so, you may not have a ton of wiggle room to negotiate pay (I always recommend you try, though). If you're going to a job that doesn't have many — or any — other people in it, companies can pay however they'd like.

Just because someone is at the same organization level doesn't mean it's a legal comparator for the Equal Pay Act. And "equal pay" doesn't mean that everyone gets paid exactly the same thing. It just requires companies to have valid reasons for pay differences (like performance or tenure or education).

And if you're in a job that's one of a kind, the company is under no obligation to pay you like anyone else, even others at the same level.

Q: The hiring process has taken SO LONG, and I finally got an offer! It took so long to get to this point, I don't

want to jinx anything by asking for more. Can I just accept the offer as-is?

A: Sure you can. But if you can hang on for just a bit longer, you might be able to negotiate a higher salary or bigger sign-on bonus. Don't let the worry of temporary discomfort turn you away from asking for what you really want. After all, negotiations can't last forever!

Q: It's clear that the company and I aren't in the same ballpark, pay-wise. What can I do to make them see reason?

A: Not much, to be honest! Because how much a company is willing to pay reflects how they value the job, it's pretty hard to move them significantly off that mark. If you're not able to come to a shared understanding of how the role should be paid, think about whether it makes sense to stop investing your time in the interview or negotiation process.

Q: I finally negotiated all of the details I wanted to with my pay package, but the recruiter doesn't want to bother with revising the offer letter. Is that okay?

A: It really isn't. Instead of waiting for them to do the right thing, take the initiative and write up the details in an email, send it to your contact, and ask them to reply with their approval. Once you get the confirmation from the company, you're good to go!

Other Awesome Stuff

Resource Reference Guide

Where to go for market pay data, state and local tax guidance, and cost of living/cost of labor information. Books I recommend. Experts you may want to consult.

Conclusion

Acknowledgements

Index

About the Author

Resource Reference Guide

Resources. You need them. Here are some of my favorites.

SALARY DATA

No salary data source is perfect. Even those awesome salary surveys compensation people use inside of organizations. It's still good to do your research — get data from multiple sources to inform your negotiations. Know, too, that a company can put any value they want on a job. You can't change that. But knowing the market will give you power in your negotiations.

Here are a few of my favorite online sources:

- Glassdoor.com
- Salary.com
- Payscale.com
- Indeed.com
- LinkedIn
- Levels.fyi
- H1bdata.info
- Careercontessa.com/resources/salary-project
- Roberthalf.com/salary-guide

If you belong to a professional organization, don't forget to check their website for salary data, too. Professional organizations often sponsor salary surveys and share results with their members.

STATE & LOCAL TAX INFO

For info about taxes in different states, search online for "tax estimator" plus the name of the state you're looking for.

COST OF LIVING/COST OF LABOR INFO

If you're looking for cost of living and cost of labor comparisons, Salary.com has some good resources.

BOOKS

If you want to know more about topics adjacent to pay negotiation, these are some of my favorite books.

- *We Have a Deal*, by Natalie Reynolds. If you want to know more about how negotiating works — from the psychology to the mindset — this book has it! And if you want to know about negotiating tactics in general, this is a great source.

- *Building a StoryBrand*, by Donald Miller. You may wonder why a branding book made my list. I love Miller's perspective on selling and marketing, which is what you're doing during the interview (and salary negotiation) process. Treating your prospective employer as the hero in their story can shift your perspective and make you even more effective.
- *When*, by Daniel Pink. This great book about timing is just plain interesting. I refer to it when I talk about ending your conversations well, but there's so much more cool stuff in the book.
- *Multipliers*, by Liz Wiseman. My all-time favorite book about leadership, this is a great one to check out when you want to be deliberate about the way you show up as a leader. When you're focusing on your leadership presence during the interview and negotiation process, *Multipliers* can help. Lots.

EXPERT ADVICE

Attorneys. You may want to bring in an attorney if you want to negotiate specific items in your employment agreement or need specific advice about equity terms. If you're joining a startup, consulting an attorney who specializes in startup equity agreements can save you a whole lot of heartache down the road.

Financial advisors. Only you know what you need from a financial perspective. A financial advisor can help you make sense of how pay changes impact your bottom line, how changing locations could affect your tax situation, or when and how to exercise equity to your greatest benefit.

Salary negotiation coaches. From recent college graduates to C-suite executives, hiring a salary negotiation coach can be a fantastic investment. When you're looking for a salary negotiation coach, make sure they understand compensation inside and out, and that they are great coaches, too. Accreditation matters. Bottom line, how and what you negotiate is your decision, and having a partner who can help you make confident, competent choices is key.

If you're interested in working one-on-one with me, please contact me at **PayUpBook@katedixon.org**.

Conclusion

This is the end...but it's only the beginning.

I hope you found this book to be helpful. And I hope you use these negotiating tips in your next salary negotiation. And the ones after that. Honing these skills will help you with negotiating in particular, and with business in general over the long haul.

I'm excited for you.

I have a confession to make. I have a bit of a different approach than many business folks. The reason I do what I do is because I believe that when people are more competent and confident, they show up more authentically, realize more of their potential, and are happier and more fulfilled. And when that happens, it's better for the world.

So by learning more about yourself, about your pay, and about negotiating, you're making the world a better place, which is exciting for me…and hopefully exciting for you, too!

I'm confident in you.

This stuff works. My clients get great results using the ***Pay UP!*** techniques and methods, which is why I'm so confident you'll do a better job now than you could have without investing the time to read this book and do the work we talked about here.

Negotiating your pay isn't easy or simple, but the more you do it, the better you'll get at it. And I'm confident you will.

Go get 'em!

Thank you so much.

This book has been a labor of love for me, and I'm grateful you've invested your time to read it.

If you find typos, please let me know — as much as my editor and I have worked to correct them, I'm sure there are some! (Although you should know that I'm a diehard fan of the Oxford Comma, and I will not be dissuaded from using it, even if you think it's improper.)

Did you enjoy ***Pay UP***? If so, please leave a review wherever you purchased the book. Reviews help readers find the books that are right for them.

For more information about my work, to subscribe to my monthly newsletter, or to read more, please visit: **www.katedixon.org/PayUpBook.**

Acknowledgements

If you've written a book, you know that it's not a solo venture; it's a monumental and collaborative undertaking. It's hard and awesome and thought-provoking and exciting and terrifying, all at the same time.

I've been wildly fortunate to have so very many people help me think about, write, and produce this book, and while it's impossible to include everyone here, I'll highlight a few...

My fantastic salary negotiation coaching clients – you inspired me in this work and helped me know what's most helpful and effective (and what may not have been helpful at all, which didn't make it into the book, thank heaven).

Those who offered advice on the craft and business of writing – thank you for sharing your insider secrets of writing and publishing. My Roving Writer colleagues kept me inspired and on track – thanks to Jess, Jeff, Marcus, Stephanie, Hildred, Jen, Bruno, and J.S. My editor, Emily Fuggetta, offered insightful feedback, and got rid of my "stuff." And the online writer communities I participate in were so generous in their advice.

My friends and colleagues – you helped me navigate the mental and emotional part of this work. Robyn Bolton, I look forward your insights, encouragement, and delicious sense of humor every week (even at 7 a.m. on Mondays!). Meg Levene and Brynn Bishop, it's a delight to share professionally and personally with you. Kasey Jones, Gina Riley, and Nina Church-Adams, your infusions of woman-power lift me up when I need it most. Corinne Dillon, Nancy Turner, Mary Morton, Monique Montanino, Sue Parham, Lisa Hunefeld, Sherry Cadsawan, Lori Giardina, Sophia Tzeng, Cynthia Escamilla, Bernice Skoro, Tammi Wheeler, Jay Lyles, Rashmi Dixit, Ellen Roney, Steven Kittinger, Lori Emerick, Debi Muchow, Sarah Graves, Jody Kennay, Arusi Couser, and Amabelle Manuel: big, big love to you.

And my wonderful, fun, and brilliant family – your support means the world to me. My parents, Betsy and Will, have shown unbridled delight with my "I made it myself!" projects from my first Christmas tree ornament (a ridiculous, paint- and sequin-encrusted Styrofoam egg) all the way to this book. My brother Jim, brother-in-law Charles, and sister Kelly have been steadfast and profuse in their cheerleading. My kids Liz and Jay are both more mystified and impressed by my work than they probably ought to be. My little dog Jeffrey sits patiently and quietly next to my desk while I write, as long as there's nobody at the door. And my husband Steve encourages me unreservedly, even when he has no clue what I'm up to.

My heart is full. Thank you all!

Index

I

L

M

N

O

P

R

S

T

V

W

About the Author

Kate Dixon is the Principal and Founder of *Dixon Consulting*, a leadership development and total rewards consultancy that specializes in salary negotiation coaching, compensation solutions, as well as workshops and teambuilding for organizations of all sizes, from startups to Fortune 100 companies.

Kate's passion is helping diverse leaders around the world accelerate their results to become more successful and more fulfilled.

Kate has spent the past 25 years working for and consulting with leaders in for-profit companies including Nike, Intel, American Express, Mercari, and Kaiser Permanente, as well as non-profits like The Learning Policy Institute, One Community Health, DePaul Industries, Period, and the Nike Community Impact Fund.

She's a certified coach, sits on the Forbes Coaches Council, and has been certified in compensation for over 20 years.

Born in Brooklyn, New York, Kate's lived all over the United States and received both her undergraduate and master's degrees from Purdue University. She lives in Portland, Oregon with her husband Steve and her little dog, Jeffrey.

Kate provides advice about leadership, culture, and organizations to subscribers at **www.katedixon.org**.

Made in the USA
Las Vegas, NV
18 December 2024

14747953R00125